CONTENTS

A NOTE ABOUT COPYRIGHT

Dear Customer

What does the little © mean and why does it matter?

Your market-leading BPP books, course materials and e-learning materials do not write and update themselves. People write them on their own behalf or as employees of an organisation that invests in this activity. Copyright law protects their livelihoods. It does so by creating rights over the use of the content.

Breach of copyright is a form of theft – as well being a criminal offence in some jurisdictions, it is potentially a serious breach of professional ethics.

With current technology, things might seem a bit hazy but, basically, without the express permission of BPP Learning Media:

- Photocopying our materials is a breach of copyright

- Scanning, ripcasting or conversion of our digital materials into different file formats, uploading them to facebook or emailing them to your friends is a breach of copyright

You can, of course, sell your books, in the form in which you have bought them – once you have finished with them. (Is this fair to your fellow students? We update for a reason). Please note the e-products are sold on a single user licence basis: we do not supply 'unlock' codes to people who have bought them secondhand.

And what about outside the UK? BPP Learning Media strives to make our materials available at prices students can afford by local printing arrangements, pricing policies and partnerships which are clearly listed on our website. A tiny minority ignore this and indulge in criminal activity by illegally photocopying our material or supporting organisations that do. If they act illegally and unethically in one area, can you really trust them?

BPP LEARNING MEDIA'S AAT MATERIALS

The AAT's assessments fall within the **Qualifications and Credit Framework** and most papers are assessed by way of an on demand **computer based assessment**. BPP Learning Media has invested heavily to ensure our materials are as relevant as possible for this method of assessment. In particular, our **suite of online resources** ensures that you are prepared for online testing by allowing you to practise numerous online tasks that are similar to the tasks you will encounter in the AAT's assessments.

Resources

The BPP range of resources comprises:

- **Texts**, covering all the knowledge and understanding needed by students, with numerous illustrations of 'how it works', practical examples and tasks for you to use to consolidate your learning. The majority of tasks within the texts have been written in an interactive style that reflects the style of the online tasks we anticipate the AAT will set. When you purchase a Text you are also granted free access to your Text content online.

- **Question Banks**, including additional learning questions plus the AAT's sample assessment(s) and a number of BPP full practice assessments. Full answers to all questions and assessments, prepared by BPP Learning Media Ltd, are included. Our question banks are provided free of charge online.

- **Passcards**, which are handy pocket-sized revision tools designed to fit in a handbag or briefcase to enable you to revise anywhere at anytime. All major points are covered in the Passcards which have been designed to assist you in consolidating knowledge.

- **Workbooks**, which have been designed to cover the units that are assessed by way of computer based project/case study. The workbooks contain many practical tasks to assist in the learning process and also a sample assessment or project to work through.

- **Lecturers' resources**, for units assessed by computer based assessments. These provide a further bank of tasks, answers and full practice assessments for classroom use, available separately only to lecturers whose colleges adopt BPP Learning Media material.

This Workbook for Professional Ethics has been written specifically to ensure comprehensive yet concise coverage of the AAT's **AQ2013** learning outcomes and assessment criteria.

Each chapter contains:

- Clear, step by step explanation of the topic
- Logical progression and linking from one chapter to the next
- Numerous illustrations of 'how it works'
- Interactive tasks within the text of the chapter itself, with answers at the back of the book. The majority of these tasks have been written in the interactive form that students can expect to see in their real assessments
- Test your learning questions of varying complexity, again with answers supplied at the back of the book. The majority of these questions have been written in the interactive form that students can expect to see in their real assessments

The emphasis in all tasks and test questions is on the practical application of the skills acquired.

Supplements

From time to time we may need to publish supplementary materials to one of our titles. This can be for a variety of reasons, from a small change in the AAT unit guidance to new legislation coming into effect between editions.

You should check our supplements page regularly for anything that may affect your learning materials. All supplements are available free of charge on our supplements page on our website at:

http://www.bpp.com/about-bpp/aboutBPP/StudentInfo#q4

Customer feedback

If you have any comments about this book, please email nisarahmed@bpp.com or write to Nisar Ahmed, AAT Head of Programme, BPP Learning Media Ltd, BPP House, Aldine Place, London W12 8AA.

Any feedback we receive is taken into consideration when we periodically update our materials, including comments on style, depth and coverage of AAT standards.

In addition, although our products pass through strict technical checking and quality control processes, unfortunately errors may occasionally slip through when producing material to tight deadlines.

When we learn of an error in a batch of our printed materials, either from internal review processes or from customers using our materials, we want to make sure customers are made aware of this as soon as possible and the appropriate action is taken to minimise the impact on student learning.

As a result, when we become aware of any such errors we will:

1) Include details of the error and, if necessary, PDF prints of any revised pages under the related subject heading on our 'supplements' page at: www.bpp.com/about-bpp/aboutBPP/StudentInfo#q4

2) Update the source files ahead of any further printing of the materials

3) Investigate the reason for the error and take appropriate action to minimise the risk of reoccurrence.

A NOTE ON TERMINOLOGY

The AAT AQ2013 standards and assessments use international terminology based on International Financial Reporting Standards (IFRSs). Although you may be familiar with UK terminology, you need to now know the equivalent international terminology for your assessments.

The following information is taken from an article on the AAT's website and compares IFRS terminology with UK GAAP terminology. It then goes on to describe the impact of IFRS terminology on students studying for each level of the AAT QCF qualification.

Note that since the article containing the information below was published, there have been changes made to some IFRSs. Therefore BPP Learning Media have updated the table and other information below to reflect these changes.

In particular, the primary performance statement under IFRSs which was formerly known as the 'income statement' or the 'statement of comprehensive income' is now called the 'statement of profit or loss' or the 'statement of profit or loss and other comprehensive income'.

What is the impact of IFRS terms on AAT assessments?

The list shown in the table that follows gives the 'translation' between UK GAAP and IFRS.

UK GAAP	IFRS
Final accounts	Financial statements
Trading and profit and loss account	**Statement of profit or loss (or statement of profit or loss and other comprehensive income)**
Turnover or Sales	Revenue or Sales Revenue
Sundry income	Other operating income
Interest payable	Finance costs
Sundry expenses	Other operating costs
Operating profit	Profit from operations
Net profit/loss	Profit/Loss for the year/period
Balance sheet	**Statement of financial position**
Fixed assets	Non-current assets
Net book value	Carrying amount
Tangible assets	Property, plant and equipment

UK GAAP	IFRS
Reducing balance depreciation	Diminishing balance depreciation
Depreciation/Depreciation expense(s)	Depreciation charge(s)
Stocks	Inventories
Trade debtors or Debtors	Trade receivables
Prepayments	Other receivables
Debtors and prepayments	Trade and other receivables
Cash at bank and in hand	Cash and cash equivalents
Trade creditors or Creditors	Trade payables
Accruals	Other payables
Creditors and accruals	Trade and other payables
Long-term liabilities	Non-current liabilities
Capital and reserves	Equity (limited companies)
Profit and loss balance	Retained earnings
Minority interest	Non-controlling interest
Cash flow statement	**Statement of cash flows**

This is certainly not a comprehensive list, which would run to several pages, but it does cover the main terms that you will come across in your studies and assessments. However, you won't need to know all of these in the early stages of your studies – some of the terms will not be used until you reach Level 4. For each level of the AAT qualification, the points to bear in mind are as follows:

Level 2 Certificate in Accounting

The IFRS terms do not impact greatly at this level. Make sure you are familiar with 'receivables' (also referred to as 'trade receivables'), 'payables' (also referred to as 'trade payables'), and 'inventories'. The terms sales ledger and purchases ledger – together with their control accounts – will continue to be used. Sometimes the control accounts might be called 'trade receivables control account' and 'trade payables control account'. The other term to be aware of is 'non-current asset' – this may be used in some assessments.

Level 3 Diploma in Accounting

At this level you need to be familiar with the term 'financial statements'. The financial statements comprise a 'statement of profit or loss' (previously known as an income statement), and a 'statement of financial position'. In the statement of profit or loss the term 'revenue' or 'sales revenue' takes the place of 'sales', and 'profit for the year' replaces 'net profit'. Other terms may be used in the statement of financial position – eg 'non-current assets' and 'carrying amount'. However, specialist limited company terms are not required at this level.

Level 4 Diploma in Accounting

At Level 4 a wider range of IFRS terms is needed, and in the case of Financial statements, are already in use – particularly those relating to limited companies. Note especially that a statement of profit or loss becomes a 'statement of profit or loss and other comprehensive income'.

Note: The information above was taken from an AAT article from the 'assessment news' area of the AAT website (www.aat.org.uk). However, it has been adapted by BPP Learning Media for changes in international terminology since the article was published.

ASSESSMENT STRATEGY

Duration

The assessment will consist of 9 tasks and 2.5 hours of time. 5 tasks will be based on a scenario in a single accountancy practice but will each have different matters to be considered. 4 tasks will be short answer questions and unrelated to that scenario.

Competency

When making assessment decisions, the assessor must exercise professional judgement in concluding whether the evidence the student has presented confirms that they are competent across the assessment criteria for the unit.

QCF Level descriptor	Summary
	Achievement at Level 3 reflects the ability to identify and use relevant understanding, methods and skills to complete tasks and address problems that, while well defined, have a measure of complexity. It includes taking responsibility for initiating and completing tasks and procedures as well as exercising autonomy and judgement within limited parameters. It also reflects awareness of different perspectives or approaches within an area of study or work.
	Knowledge and understanding
	▪ Use factual, procedural and theoretical understanding to complete tasks and address problems that, while well defined, may be complex and non-routine.
	▪ Interpret and evaluate relevant information and ideas.
	▪ Be aware of the nature of the area of study or work.
	▪ Have awareness of different perspectives or approaches within the area of study or work.
	Application and action
	▪ Address problems that, while well defined, may be complex and non-routine.
	▪ Identify, select and use appropriate skills, methods and procedures.
	▪ Use appropriate investigation to inform actions.
	▪ Review how effective methods and actions have been.

Autonomy and accountability

- Take responsibility for initiating and completing tasks and procedures, including, where relevant, responsibility for supervising or guiding others.

- Exercise autonomy and judgement within limited parameters.

Students will be assessed by completion of a computer-based project, consisting of nine tasks, which will include a broad range of topics across the assessment criteria for this unit.

Five tasks will each require a more discursive response. These will be based on a scenario in a single accountancy practice but will each have different matters to be considered, some of which may involve accountants in business as well as in practice. Four tasks will be short answer questions and unrelated to that organisation.

The purpose of the assessment as a whole is to assess whether students are competent in knowing, understanding, applying, acting on and resolving ethical and sustainability issues for accounting and finance professionals in the workplace. The tasks requiring more discursive responses will in addition assess the ability of the student to review information autonomously, to exercise professional judgement and to express an opinion for which they will be accountable.

Guidance for assessors for AAT assessments will include sufficient guidance to enable the assessors to confidently derive Competent and Not Yet Competent performance decisions. When making assessment decisions, the assessor must use their professional judgement when concluding whether they are satisfied that the evidence the student has presented confirms that they are competent across the assessment criteria for the unit.

Students judged competent will demonstrate:

- Knowledge and understanding of the topics covered in the professional ethics unit.

- Clear communication of the nature of professional ethics and sustainability, and how these concepts are applied in the workplace.

- Appropriate evaluation and interpretation of the issues raised in a defined scenario.

- Awareness of the different challenges that face accountants in practice as opposed to those in business.

	• Application of knowledge and understanding to complex and non-routine problems, within limited parameters.
	• Appropriate investigation of issues arising in problems so that informed action is taken.
	• Thoughtful review processes of the effectiveness of actions taken/recommended.
	• Ability to tackle problems independently.
	• Willingness to take responsibility for recommending, initiating and completing actions.
	• Exercise of professional judgement in formulating responses to problems.

AAT UNIT GUIDE

Professional Ethics (PETH)

Introduction

Please note that this document is subject to annual review and revision to ensure that it accurately reflects the assessment criteria.

This guidance relates to the Level 3 unit Professional Ethics. It should be read in conjunction with the standards for this unit. The aim of this guidance is to provide further detail and additional advice for tutors delivering the Professional Ethics unit of the AAT Level 3 qualification. This guidance includes detail on the topics covered within the unit, and the depth and breadth to which these topics need to be taught and learnt. Only topics described and covered within this guidance will be assessed.

Professional Ethics is an entirely knowledge-based unit which seeks to ensure that students have an excellent understanding of the principles of ethical working, of what is meant by ethical behaviour when working with internal and external customers, of when and how to take appropriate action following any suspected breaches of ethical codes, and of the ethical responsibility of the accounting and finance professional in promoting sustainability.

Knowledge of ethical and sustainable values is first introduced into AAT's accounting qualification in the Level 2 unit Work Effectively in Accounting and Finance. Ethics and sustainability are much more fully covered and set very firmly in the context of accounting and finance in this Professional Ethics unit at Level 3. At Level 4 the topics are extended further in the Internal Control and Accounting Systems unit, to include the skill of conducting ethical and sustainability evaluations of an accounting system.

The purpose of the unit

This knowledge unit recognises the importance of ethics and sustainability in modern business organisations, and that the student must act and work in an ethical manner. Its purpose is to support students in:

- Working within the ethical code applicable to accounting and finance professionals.

- Ensuring the public has a good level of confidence in accounting practices or functions.

- Protecting their own and their organisation's professional reputation and integrity.

- Upholding principles of sustainability.

Learning objectives

In this Professional Ethics unit students develop an understanding of the importance of ethics and sustainability in the modern organisation. This involves first of all recognising the principles on which good behaviour at work is based and understanding what is meant by ethical behaviour. Students then need to know when to take action on suspicions or knowledge of unethical behaviour or non-compliance with laws and regulations. In addition, the student must appreciate how to uphold the principles of sustainability in the workplace. This understanding protects the professional reputation and integrity of both the student and their organisation, and enhances the public's level of confidence in accounting practices and accounting functions.

Learning outcomes

This unit consists of four learning outcomes.

- Understand principles of ethical working.

- Understand ethical behaviour when working with internal and external customers.

- Understand when and how to take appropriate action following suspected breaches of ethical codes.

- Understand the ethical responsibility of the finance professional in promoting sustainability.

Learning Outcome	Assessment Criteria	Covered in Chapter
1 Understand principles of ethical working	1.1 Explain these fundamental principles of ethical behaviour: integrity, objectivity, professional and technical competence and due care, confidentiality, professional behaviour	1
	1.2 Outline the relevant legal, regulatory and ethical requirements affecting the accounting and finance sector	1
	1.3 Explain the role of professional bodies in relation to the accounting and finance sector	1
	1.4 Explain why individuals, organisations or industry sectors are expected to operate within codes of conduct and practice	1

Learning Outcome	Assessment Criteria	Covered in Chapter
	1.5 Explain the risks of improper practice to an organisation and the importance of vigilance	1
	1.6 Identify opportunities for maintaining an up-to-date knowledge of changes to codes of practice, regulation and legislation affecting the accounting and finance sector	1
2 Understand ethical behaviour when working with internal and external customers	2.1 Explain how to act ethically when working with clients, suppliers, colleagues and others	1, 2
	2.2 Explain the importance of objectivity and maintaining a professional distance between professional duties and personal life at all times	1, 2, 3
	2.3 Explain the importance of adhering to organisational and professional values, codes of practice and regulations	1
	2.4 Explain the importance of adhering to organisational policies for handling clients' monies	3
	2.5 Identify circumstances when confidential information should be disclosed and who is entitled to the information	3
	2.6 Explain the importance of working within the limits and confines of one's own professional experience, knowledge and expertise	3
3 Understand when and how to take appropriate action following suspected breaches of ethical codes	3.1 Identify the relevant authorities and internal departments to which unethical behaviour, breaches of confidentiality, suspected illegal acts or other malpractice should be reported	3
	3.2 Identify the appropriate action to take in instances when requests for work are beyond the employee's competence	3

Learning Outcome	Assessment Criteria	Covered in Chapter
	3.3 Identify inappropriate client behaviour and how to report it	4
	3.4 Explain the internal and external reporting procedures which should be followed if an employee suspects an employer, colleague or client has committed, or may commit, an act which is believed to be illegal or unethical	4
	3.5 Outline strategies that could be used to prevent ethical conflict	4
4 Understand the ethical responsibility of the finance professional in promoting sustainability	4.1 Explain the importance of an ethical approach to sustainability	1
	4.2 Outline the responsibilities of finance professionals in upholding the principles of sustainability	1

Delivery guidance

When teaching this unit, tutors must stress the relevance and value of all four learning outcomes to all students, since the assessment will cover all the assessment criteria set out below, including a range of topics within each assessment criterion.

Students should be encouraged to become familiar with the key points of the ethical code for professional accountants over the course of delivery of the unit. In particular, they require specific knowledge of the ethical code in relation to:

- The objectives of the accountancy profession
- The purposes of the ethical code for professional accountants
- The detailed meaning of each of the fundamental principles
- The types of threat and safeguard available
- The ethical conflict resolution process
- Disclosure of confidential information

AAT's Code of Professional Ethics should be taken as exemplar of the ethical code for professional accountants.

Note that the Appendix to this guidance contains details of the relevant knowledge required of students in respect of money laundering and managing client monies.

1. Understand principles of ethical working

1.1 Explain these fundamental principles of ethical behaviour: integrity, objectivity, professional and technical competence and due care, confidentiality, professional behaviour

- Explain what is meant by each of the fundamental principles of ethical behaviour found in the ethical code for professional accountants:

  - Integrity
  - Objectivity
  - Professional (and technical) competence and due care
  - Confidentiality
  - Professional behaviour

1.2 Outline the relevant legal, regulatory and ethical requirements affecting the accounting and finance sector

- Explain the relevant distinctions between civil and criminal law.

  - Civil law results in a claim in a civil court by a claimant against a defendant to enforce rights that arose between them (under contract, negligence and trust); there is no involvement by the state. The consequence is not punishment of the party who loses but some form of compensation for the party who wins.

  - Criminal law results in a prosecution in a criminal court by the state of the accused for a breach of the law, such as for the crimes of theft, money laundering, terrorist financing, bribery and fraud. The consequence is punishment of the accused, if found guilty, by imprisonment or a fine.

- Explain the importance of compliance with the law, with other regulations and with ethical codes.

- State the legal status of a professional accountancy body's ethical code and its application to accountants in practice and accountants in business.

- Explain that professional accountants are held to account by professional bodies for breaches of their ethical codes.

- Identify the limits of the ethical code for professional accountants and explain that additional regulations apply.

- Explain that other forms of regulation affect professionals in the accounting and finance sector, namely employment protection and equality laws, and health and safety regulations.

- Explain the objectives of the accountancy profession as stated in the ethical code for professional accountants, including acknowledgement of a public interest duty to society as well as to the client or employer.

- Explain the distinction in accounting and finance between statutory regulated functions (the 'reserved areas' of audit, investment business and insolvency) and other professional activities (accounting and tax).

- Outline the methods by which the accountancy and finance profession is regulated, including:

    - The role of professional accountancy bodies in regulating their members in general, and in relation to the reserved areas and supervision for money laundering/terrorist financing.

    - The structure of the regulation of the main professional accountancy bodies in the UK.

1.3 Explain the role of professional bodies in relation to the accounting and finance sector

- Explain the nature and role of, and relationship between, bodies that are relevant to the professional accountant's work, including AAT, sponsoring bodies of AAT, other professional accountancy bodies in the UK and its member bodies, and IFAC.

- Explain that a person may offer services as an accountant in the UK without membership of a professional accountancy body. However for money laundering purposes accountants who are not supervised by a professional accountancy body must register as accountancy service providers with HMRC.

- Identify IFAC's International Ethics Standards Board for Accountants (IESBA) as the body setting the basic ethical code for professional accountants that underlies the ethical codes of the various professional accountancy bodies.

- Explain the nature and role of HMRC and the National Crime Agency (NCA) in relation to the accounting and finance sector.

1.4 Explain why individuals, organisations or industry sectors are expected to operate within codes of conduct and practice

- Specify the basics of business ethics (in addition to professional ethics), namely codes of principles and values that govern decisions and actions within an organisation, including corporate culture and the impact of the 'tone at the top' on corporate culture.

- Explain the legal status of codes of conduct/codes of practice in general, including organisation-specific ethical codes, and voluntary and statutory industry sector codes.

- Explain the objectives and functions of codes of conduct/codes of practice.

- Explain why individuals, organisations and industries should operate within such codes.

- Explain the differences between a principles-based approach and a rules-based approach to ethics, conduct and practice.

1.5 Explain the risks of improper practice to an organisation and the importance of vigilance

- Outline what is meant by risk for an organisation.

- Classify types of operational risk that arise from improper practice in an organisation into reputational, process, people, systems, legal and event (physical, social, political and economic) risks.

- Explain the risks to an organisation of unethical behaviour by its managers and employees, and the importance of vigilance by professional accountants in preventing and detecting this.

- Explain the money laundering and terrorist financing offences and their consequences for accountancy service providers and organisations (see Appendix to this document).

- Explain the risk to an organisation of becoming involved in money laundering or terrorist financing, and the importance of vigilance by accountancy service providers in preventing and detecting this.

- Outline how procedures for customer due diligence should be applied to new and existing clients by accountancy service providers in practice, in accordance with the Money Laundering Regulations (see Appendix to this document).

- Explain the basic requirement on organisations to comply with the Bribery Act, and the penalties for non-compliance by an organisation.

1.6 Identify opportunities for maintaining an up-to-date knowledge of changes to codes of practice, regulation and legislation affecting the accounting and finance sector

- Explain that having up-to-date technical knowledge means the professional accountant can act with technical and professional competence in providing services to clients and service to an employer.

- Identify the areas in which up-to-date technical knowledge for a professional accountant is critical, namely: reporting and auditing standards; ethical codes; tax and companies legislation; relevant criminal law including bribery, fraud and money laundering; regulation of accounting, reporting, tax compliance, audit and regulation of the accounting and finance profession.

- Explain how a professional accountant may keep up-to-date with technical changes, namely reading professional journals, enrolling on update courses, complying with continuing professional development (CPD) requirements for qualified professional accountants.

2. Understand ethical behaviour when working with internal and external customers

2.1 Explain how to act ethically when working with clients, suppliers, colleagues and others

- Describe what is meant by ethical behaviour, especially in relation to integrity and avoidance by a professional accountant of association with misleading information.

- Explain that ethical behaviour is required at all times when working with clients, suppliers, colleagues and others in order to comply with the ethical principles.

- Distinguish between behaviour that is ethical and appropriate in a given set of circumstances, and behaviour that is unethical and inappropriate.

- Explain how the conceptual framework is designed to operate in relation to acting within the five fundamental ethical principles, and the importance of using professional judgement.

- Explain the types of threat to ethical principles (self-interest, self-review, advocacy, familiarity and intimidation).

- Explain the types of safeguard that are used by professional accountants to address threats to the fundamental principles in a given set of circumstances, and what to do when a threat cannot be eliminated or reduced to an acceptable level.

- Explain what is meant by professional behaviour that is compliant with the law, and that reflects well on the accounting and finance profession, including the importance of appearing to act ethically in the view of a third party.

2.2 Explain the importance of objectivity and maintaining a professional distance between professional duties and personal life at all times

- Describe what is meant by objectivity for a professional accountant.

- Explain how an accountant in practice should aim to maintain objectivity in all services.

- Explain what an accountant in practice should do about conflicts of interest.

- Explain what an accountant in business should do about conflicts of interest, and threats arising from financial interests, compensation and incentives linked to financial reporting and decision-making.

- Explain how professional accountants should deal with the threats to objectivity from accepting gifts, hospitality and inducements.

- State the Bribery Act offences for individuals and the penalties for giving and receiving bribes.

2.3 Explain the importance of adhering to organisational and professional values, codes of practice and regulations

- Explain the purposes of the ethical code for professional accountants, namely: setting out required standards of professional behaviour and how to achieve them; protection of the public interest; maintenance of the professional accountancy body's reputation.

- Explain key organisational values, including complying with regulations in spirit as well as to the letter with regard to: being transparent with customers and suppliers; reporting financial and regulatory information clearly and on time; when to accept and give gifts and hospitality; paying suppliers a fair price and on time; providing fair treatment, decent wages and good working conditions to employees.

- Explain the effect of voluntary and statutory codes of practice and regulations on organisations and individuals.

- Explain the consequences for organisations of non-compliance with values, codes and regulations for example, regulatory fines.

- Explain when disciplinary action by the relevant professional accountancy body can be brought against an accountant for misconduct (bringing the profession into disrepute, breach of applicable regulations) and the possible penalties that can arise (including expulsion or fines).

- Explain that internal disciplinary procedures may be brought against the accountant by the employer.

- Explain the importance of professional accountants upholding the values of sustainability and corporate social responsibility in the public interest.

2.4 Explain the importance of adhering to organisational policies for handling clients' monies

- Explain the issues surrounding, and appropriate policies for, an accountant in practice handling clients' monies (see Appendix to this document).

- Describe the potential consequences for an accountant in practice of non-compliance with policies for handling clients' monies in relation to: action by the professional body; action by the client for breach of trust/contract; money laundering (see Appendix to this document);

breach of investment business rules; fraud (Fraud Act 2006 offences); theft.

2.5 Identify circumstances when confidential information should be disclosed and who is entitled to the information

- Specify the meaning and importance of confidentiality, including both the fundamental principle and the legal rules (Data Protection Act 1998 and registration with the authorities as a data user).

- Explain the types of situation that present threats to confidentiality.

- Explain when a professional accountant may be justified in disclosing confidential information.

- Identify from a given set of circumstances the appropriate course of action regarding disclosure of confidential information.

- Identify from a given set of circumstances the appropriate person/organisation to whom disclosure should be made.

2.6 Explain the importance of working within the limits and confines of one's own professional experience, knowledge and expertise

- Explain the consequences of a professional accountant failing to work within the limits of their professional expertise, namely: breach of contract in the supply of services, professional negligence; breach of trust; accusations of fraud.

- Explain the importance of an accountant in practice working within the confines of their own professional experience, knowledge and expertise, and of the client engagement.

- Explain the dangers for an accountant in practice of giving references for clients or third parties in the absence of full knowledge.

- Explain the purpose and likely effectiveness of an accountant in practice issuing a disclaimer of liability.

3. Understand when and how to take appropriate action following suspected breaches of ethical codes

3.1 Identify the relevant authorities and internal departments to which unethical behaviour, breaches of confidentiality, suspected illegal acts or other malpractice should be reported

- Describe the relevant authorities to which reports about suspected illegal acts should be made, namely:

  - Money Laundering Reporting Officer (MLRO) or National Crime Agency (NCA) regarding money laundering and terrorist financing.

  - MLRO/NCA regarding tax errors.

- Other relevant authorities in the UK and elsewhere, including HMRC and the police.

- Identify any prescribed internal department and/or external professional body to which reports should be made regarding unethical behaviour, breaches of confidentiality or malpractice.

- Identify, in a given circumstance, the appropriate persons charged with governance of the organisation, such as the board of directors or the audit committee, to which a report should be made.

3.2 Identify the appropriate action to take in instances when requests for work are beyond the employee's competence

- Explain the type of concern that may arise for a professional accountant about being asked to complete work for which they do not have sufficient expertise, time, training and/or support.

- Identify from a set of circumstances the appropriate time at which advice about such concerns should be sought from an employer's confidential helpline or that of an appropriate professional body.

- Explain what an accountant in practice should do if requested to complete work outside the confines of their own professional experience, expertise or competence in a given set of circumstances.

- Explain what an accountant in business should do if requested to complete tasks for which they do not have sufficient expertise.

3.3 Identify inappropriate client behaviour and how to report it

- Explain the type of concern that may arise for an accountant in practice about inappropriate client behavior.

- Explain the consequences for an accountancy service provider of failing to act appropriately in response to such behaviour, including the potential for the offences of 'tipping off' and 'failure to disclose'.

- Explain the relevance of the crime of 'prejudicing an investigation' to all persons.

- Specify the key threats to the ethical principles that arise for an accountant in practice from inappropriate client behaviour (familiarity, intimidation and advocacy threats) and the safeguards which could be put in place to mitigate them.

- Identify from a set of circumstances when and how advice about inappropriate client behaviour should be sought from the helpline of either the appropriate professional body or the firm of the accountant in practice.

- State how to report inappropriate client behaviour.

3.4 Explain the internal and external reporting procedures which should be followed if an employee suspects an employer, colleague or client has committed, or may commit, an act which is believed to be illegal or unethical

- Identify what to do if a breach of the ethical code for professional accountants has taken place.

- State what should be reported by accountancy service providers making required disclosures in either internal reports or suspicious activity reports regarding the illegal acts of money laundering/terrorist financing under the Proceeds of Crime Act 2002 and money laundering regulations (see Appendix to this document).

- State the nature of the protection given by protected disclosures and authorised disclosures under these rules.

- State the position of accountants in business regarding external reporting of the employer's illegal activities under these rules when the accountant in business is directly involved and also when they are not directly involved.

- Explain the internal whistleblowing reporting procedures that may be available if an employee suspects an employer, colleague or client has committed, or may commit, an act which is believed to be illegal or unethical.

- Explain the protection offered to external whistle-blowers by the Public Interest Disclosure Act.

3.5 Outline strategies that could be used to prevent ethical conflict

- Explain how ethical conflict situations could arise in practice and in business.

- Explain how documented policies on various issues can be used as safeguards to prevent ethical conflict from arising.

- Explain the stages in the process for ethical conflict resolution when a situation presents a conflict in application of the fundamental principles, as set out in the ethical code for accountants.

4. Understand the ethical responsibility of the finance professional in promoting sustainability

4.1 Explain the importance of an ethical approach to sustainability

- Explain that professional accountants have a public interest duty to protect society as a whole so must consider: the economic/financial, social and environmental aspects of their work in order to support sustainability and sustainable development; the long-term responsible management of resource use by their organisation; facilitating the

running of their organisation in a sustainable manner; the risks to an organisation, and to society as a whole, of not acting sustainably.

- Explain that sustainable development is part of an organisation's corporate social responsibility (CSR).

4.2 Outline the responsibilities of finance professionals in upholding the principles of sustainability

Students must be able to explain the importance of professional accountants being involved in:

- Creating and promoting an ethics-based culture that discourages unethical or illegal practices, including money laundering, terrorist financing, fraud, theft, bribery, non-compliance with applicable regulations, bullying and short-term decision-making.

- Remaining objective while championing that organisations must aim to 'meet the needs of the present without compromising the ability of future generations to meet their own needs' (the sustainability definition used in the UN's Brundtland Report).

- Evaluating and quantifying reputational and other ethical risks.

- Taking social, environmental and economic/financial factors (the 'triple bottom line') into account when measuring position and performance, and when assisting with decision-making, so that sustainable development is encouraged.

- Promoting sustainable practices through the organisation in relation to products and services, customers, employees, the workplace, the supply chain and business functions and processes.

- Raising awareness of social responsibility and the need to consider the impact of decisions and actions on sustainability.

The assessment

Task	Learning outcome	Assessment criteria	Topics within task range
1	LO1	LO1.2, LO1.3	Legal, regulatory and ethical environment of the accounting and finance sector, including the role of professional bodies
2	LO1, LO2, LO3	LO1.6, LO2.1, LO2.6, LO3.2	Technical and professional competence and due care, and professional behaviour, including the scope of the professional accountant's work and the importance of working within their range of professional expertise
3	LO2	LO2.4	Handling clients' monies
4	LO2	LO2.5	Disclosure of confidential information
5	LO1, LO2	LO1.1, LO2.1	Fundamental principles of ethical behaviour and their application in the workplace
6	LO1, LO2	LO1.4, LO1.5, LO2.3	Organisational values and organisation/industry codes of practice and regulations, including why organisations and individuals should act in line with values and within both the law and relevant codes
7	LO2, LO3	LO2.2, LO3.5	Objectivity and the prevention and resolution of ethical conflicts and conflicts of interest
8	LO3	LO3.1, LO3.3, LO3.4	Taking appropriate action following suspected breaches of ethical codes and inappropriate or illegal behaviour by clients, colleagues or employers
9	LO2, LO4	LO2.3, LO4.1, LO4.2	Upholding sustainability and CSR in the public interest

APPENDIX TO UNIT GUIDANCE FOR PROFESSIONAL ETHICS (PETH)

Contents

Money laundering
Managing client monies

MONEY LAUNDERING

What are money laundering and terrorist financing?

Money laundering involves the proceeds of crime while terrorist financing may involve both legitimate property and the proceeds of crime.

Money laundering is the process by which criminally obtained money or other assets (criminal property) are exchanged for 'clean' money or other assets with no obvious link to their criminal origins. It also covers money, however come by, which is used to fund terrorism.

Criminal property is property which was obtained as a result of criminal conduct and the person knows or suspects that it was obtained from such conduct. It may take any form, including money or money's worth, securities, tangible property and intangible property.

Activities related to money laundering include:

- Acquiring, using or possessing criminal property.
- Handling the proceeds of crimes such as theft, fraud and tax evasion.
- Being knowingly involved in any way with criminal or terrorist property.
- Entering into arrangements to facilitate laundering criminal or terrorist property.
- Investing the proceeds of crimes in other financial products.
- Investing the proceeds of crimes through the acquisition of property/assets.
- Transferring criminal property.

Terrorist financing is fund raising, possessing or dealing with property or facilitating someone else to do so, when intending, knowing or suspecting or having reasonable cause to suspect that it is intended for the purposes of terrorism.

Terrorist property is money or property likely to be used for terrorist purposes or the proceeds of commissioning or carrying out terrorist acts.

What are the money laundering and terrorist financing offences?

The statutory definition of money laundering is 'an act which constitutes an offence under sections 327, 328 or 329 of POCA'.

These three money laundering offences are:

- s327 – Concealing, disguising, converting, transferring or removing criminal property.

- s328 – Taking part in an arrangement to facilitate the acquisition, use or control of criminal property.

- s329 – Acquiring, using or possessing criminal property.

Terrorism is the use or threat of action designed to influence government, or to intimidate any section of the public, or to advance a political, religious or ideological cause where the action would involve violence, threats to health and safety, damage to property or disruption of electronic systems.

The definition of 'terrorist property' means that all dealings with funds or property which are likely to be used for the purposes of terrorism, even if the funds are 'clean' in origin, are a terrorist financing offence.

There are no 'de minimis' exceptions in relation to either money laundering or terrorist financing offences.

Defences available to any person involved in money laundering offences and/or similar offences under TA 2000 include making an 'authorised disclosure' to the appropriate authorities.

The maximum penalty for money laundering or terrorist financing is 14 years imprisonment or an unlimited fine.

The UK legislation on money laundering and terrorist financing applies to the proceeds of conduct that are a criminal offence in the UK and most conduct occurring elsewhere that would have been an offence if it had taken place in the UK.

UK Anti-Money Laundering Legislation (AMLL)

The AMLL consist of:

- The Proceeds of Crime Act 2002 as amended (POCA)
- The Terrorism Act 2000 as amended (TA)
- Money Laundering Regulations 2007 (MLR)

To whom does the AMLL apply?

The three money laundering offences under POCA and the similar offences under TA can be committed by **any person**.

However, POCA and TA include additional offences which can be committed by **individuals working in the regulated sector**, which is by people providing specified professional services such as accountancy. This means that an **accountant** (ie an AAT member in practice) will be personally liable for breaching POCA and TA if he or she acts as an accountancy service provider while turning a 'blind eye' to a client's suspect dealings.

The MLR impose duties on 'relevant persons' (sole traders and firms (not employees) operating within the regulated sector) to establish and maintain practice, policies and procedures to detect and deter activities relating to money laundering and terrorist financing. It is the sole trader or firm which will be liable therefore for any breach of the MLR.

The practice, policies and procedures required by the MLR of accountancy service providers include:

- Customer due diligence on clients
- Reporting money laundering/terrorist financing
- Record keeping

Customer due diligence (CDD) on clients

Timing of CDD

CDD must be applied by accountants in practice to all new clients **before** services are provided to them and at appropriate times to existing clients on a risk-sensitive basis.

The one exception to this is where to do so would interrupt the normal conduct of business and there is little risk of money laundering or terrorist financing, in which case the accountant must always:

- Find out who the client claims to be before commencing the client's instructions and

- Complete CDD as soon as reasonably possible afterwards.

MLR state that CDD must be applied in the following situations:

- When establishing a business relationship

- When carrying out an occasional transaction (ie involving 15,000 (euros) or the equivalent in sterling or more)

- Where there is a suspicion of money laundering or terrorist financing or

- Where there are doubts about previously obtained customer identification information.

Elements of CDD for new clients

There are three elements to CDD for new clients:

1. Find out who the client claims to be – name, address, date of birth – and obtain evidence to check that the client is as claimed.

2. Obtain evidence so the accountant is satisfied that he or she knows who any beneficial owners are. This means beneficial owners must be considered on an individual basis. Generally, a beneficial owner is an individual who ultimately owns 25% or more of the client or the transaction property.

3. Obtain information on the purpose and intended nature of the transaction.

The evidence obtained can be documentary, data or information from a reliable and independent source, or a mix of all of these.

If CDD cannot be completed, **the accountant must not act for the client** – and should consider whether to submit an Internal Report or Suspicious Activity Report, as appropriate (see below).

On-going monitoring of existing clients

On-going monitoring must be applied to existing clients. This means that an accountant must:

- Carry out appropriate and risk-sensitive CDD measures to any transaction which appears to be inconsistent with knowledge of the client or the client's business or risk profile. For example, if a client suddenly has an injection of significant funds, check the source of funds. If a beneficial owner is revealed, obtain evidence of the beneficial owner's identity and the nature and purpose of the injection of the funds.

- Keep CDD documents, data and information up to date. For example, if a client company has a change to its directorship, update records accordingly.

Reporting money laundering/terrorist financing

Accountant's duty to report

POCA and TA impose an obligation on accountants (individuals within the regulated sector, including those involved in providing accountancy services to clients ie AAT members in practice), to submit in defined circumstances:

1. An Internal Report to a Money Laundering Reporting Officer (MLRO), by those employed in a group practice.

2. A Suspicious Activity Report (SAR) to the National Crime Agency (NCA), by sole practitioners and MLROs.

There are two circumstances (subject to exceptions, below) when a required disclosure in an internal report or a SAR, collectively referred to below as a report, must be made by an accountant:

1. When the accountant wishes to provide services in relation to property which it is actually known or suspected relates to money laundering or terrorist financing. In such circumstances, the reporter must indicate in the report that consent is required to provide such services, and must refrain from doing so until consent is received.

2. When the accountant actually knows or suspects, or there are reasonable (objective) grounds for knowing or suspecting, that another person is engaged in money laundering or terrorist financing, whether or not he or she wishes to act for such person. The person in question could be a client, a colleague or a third party.

'Failure to disclose' offence for accountants

It is an offence for an accountant to fail to disclose a suspicion or knowledge of money laundering.

The maximum penalty for failure to disclose is five years imprisonment or an unlimited fine.

Exceptions to the duty to report

The obligation of an accountant to report does NOT apply if:

1. The information which forms the basis of knowledge or suspicion or the reasonable grounds to know or suspect was obtained other than in the course of the accountant's business, for example, on a social occasion.

2. The information came about in privileged circumstances, that is in order for the accountant to provide legal advice, such as explaining a client's tax liability (except when it is judged that the advice has been sought to enable the client to commit a criminal offence or avoid detection) or expert opinion or services in relation to actual or contemplated legal proceedings.

3. There is a reasonable excuse for not reporting, in which case the report must be made as soon as reasonable in the circumstances.

Contents of the report: required disclosure

The internal report or SAR must contain, at a minimum, the required disclosure of:

- The identity of the suspect (if known);
- The information or other matter on which the knowledge or suspicion of money laundering (or reasonable grounds for such) is based; and
- The whereabouts of the laundered property (if known).

Reports made under POCA are either protected disclosures or authorised disclosures:

Effect of a report: protected disclosure

Any report providing the required disclosure which is made by any person, not just an accountant, forming a money laundering suspicion, at work or when carrying out professional activities (whether or not providing accountancy services to clients), is a protected disclosure. This means the person is protected against allegations of breach of confidentiality; however the restriction on disclosure of information was imposed.

Note. Any individual, business or organisation may make a voluntary protected disclosure; it is only in the regulated sector that such reports are compulsory.

Effect of a report: authorised disclosure

Any person who realises they may have engaged in or be about to engage in money laundering should make what is known as an authorised disclosure to the appropriate authority. This may provide a defence against charges of money laundering provided it is made before the act is carried out (and NCA's consent to the act is obtained), or it is made as soon as possible on the initiative of that person after the act is done and with good reason being shown for the delay (eg the person did not realise criminal property was involved and made the report on their own initiative as soon as this was suspected/known).

'Tipping off' offence for accountants

Once an accountant has made a report, or has become aware that a report has been made*, a criminal offence is committed if information is disclosed that is likely to prejudice any actual or contemplated investigation following the report. The person making the disclosure does not have to intend to prejudice an investigation for this offence to apply.

*__Note__. The report does not have to have been made by the person making the tip-off; that person merely needs to know or suspect that one has been made to a MLRO, NCA, HMRC or the police.

The maximum penalty for tipping off is five years imprisonment or an unlimited fine.

'Prejudicing an investigation' offence for all persons

An offence may be committed where any person (not just an accountant):

- Knows or suspects that a money laundering investigation is being conducted or is about to be conducted; and

- Makes a disclosure which is likely to prejudice the investigation; or

- Falsifies, conceals or destroys documents relevant to the investigation, or causes that to happen.

The person making the disclosure does not have to intend to prejudice an investigation for this offence to apply. However, there is a defence available if the person making the disclosure did not know or suspect the disclosure would be prejudicial, did not know or suspect the documents were relevant, or did not intend to conceal any facts from the person carrying out the investigation.

MANAGING CLIENT MONIES

Accountants in practice are prohibited from holding monies related to investments unless they are authorised to do so under the Financial Services and Markets Act 2000.

What are client monies?

Client monies are any funds, or form of documents of title to money, or documents of title which can be converted into money that an accountant in practice holds on behalf of his or her client. This does not include any sum that is immediately due and payable on demand, for example the accountant in practice's fees for work done or fees paid in advance for work to be done.

Client monies do not include the use and control of a client's own bank account. However, where an accountant in practice has control of the client's own bank account, the client's specific written authority must have been obtained and acknowledged by the client's bank before the professional accountant in practice exercises any control over such bank account and adequate records of the transactions undertaken must be maintained.

Examples of items that will normally constitute client monies include:

- HMRC refunds received on behalf of clients.

- Funds entrusted to a professional accountant in practice by the client to assist in carrying out the client's instructions.

- Surplus funds that fall at the end of an engagement.

How and when to hold client monies

Where an accountant in practice holds client monies, such monies are held in trust and the accountant is acting as a trustee and must be prepared to account to the client upon request. Failure to properly account could result in criminal and/or civil proceedings for theft and/or abuse of position.

Client monies cannot be held in certain circumstances, including:

- Where the accountant in practice knows or suspects the monies represent criminal property or are to be used for illegal activities.

- Where there is no justification for holding the monies, for example the monies do not relate to a service the accountant in practice provides.

- Where a condition on the accountant in practice's licence or registration prohibits dealing with client monies.

The following are conditions that apply when a professional accountant in practice holds client monies:

- The monies must be kept separately from personal monies or monies belonging to the practice.

- The monies must only be used for the purpose for which they were intended.

- The monies must be held in the same currency that it was received unless the client has given instructions to exchange into another currency.

- The accountant must ensure that the client has been identified and verified on a risk-sensitive basis before holding monies on their behalf.

- The accountant must be ready at all times to account for those monies or any income, dividends or gains generated on them, to the client or any persons entitled to such accounting.

chapter 1:
THE PRINCIPLES OF ETHICAL WORKING

chapter coverage 📖

In this opening chapter, we consider the fundamental principles of ethical behaviour as they apply in the general context of the UK accountancy profession, sustainability and other issues that affect the ethical accountant such as disciplinary action and continuing professional development.

The topics covered are:

- ✍ What are ethics?
- ✍ What does acting ethically look like?
- ✍ The role of an accountant
- ✍ Why behave ethically?
- ✍ Fundamental ethical principles
- ✍ The conceptual framework
- ✍ Principles versus rules
- ✍ Compliance with the law
- ✍ The accountancy profession
- ✍ Codes of conduct and codes of practice
- ✍ Business ethics and professional values
- ✍ Sustainability and corporate social responsibility
- ✍ Duties and responsibilities of finance professionals in relation to sustainability
- ✍ Risks from improper practice
- ✍ Disciplinary action by a professional body and employer
- ✍ Continuing professional development (CPD)

WHAT ARE ETHICS?

Ethics are a set of moral principles that guide behaviour.

Ethical values are assumptions and beliefs about what constitutes 'right' and 'wrong' behaviour.

Individuals have **personal ethics**, often reflecting the beliefs of the families, cultures and educational **environments** in which they developed their ideas.

Organisations also have ethical values, based on the **norms and standards of behaviour** that their leaders believe will best help them express their identity and achieve their objectives.

The society we live in could not exist without **rules and standards**. Think about it, what would life be like if everyone went about doing exactly what they felt like?

People may decide not to turn up for work. This would mean shops not opening, and that you could not buy food. What we consider crime would spiral out of control as members of the public decide to take what they want and the police would only tackle criminals if they felt like it. Businesses would not function and the financial markets could not operate.

As society developed from prehistoric tribes to the complex interrelationships we have today, **rules regulating behaviour** had to evolve also. This is because humans recognised the need for everyone to work together for the good of the group.

Ethics and morals are concerned with **right and wrong** and how conduct should be judged to be good or bad. It is about how we should live our lives and, in particular, how we should behave towards other people. It is therefore relevant to all forms of human activity.

WHAT DOES ACTING ETHICALLY LOOK LIKE?

As an accountant you will have your own views of what is ethical and it may differ slightly from the **views of others.** However, most people share broadly similar views about what is right and wrong. For example, ideas of honesty, fairness, sensitivity, loyalty, trust and hard work are often shared.

There are often several strands of an individual's ethics, We have already seen **personal ethics**, but **professional** and **business ethics** also play a part.

Professional ethics

Professional ethics are the views and rules of the professional organisation that an individual is a member of. In the case of an accountant it is usually the rules and views of the organisation that they are a member of, such as the AAT, ACCA, ICAEW or CIMA.

You should note that it is perfectly possible for an individual to find an action to be **justified ethically** (in terms of professional ethics) **but be immoral** (to their personal views).

Key reasons for **accountants** to behave **ethically**:

- Ethical issues may be a matter of law and regulation and accountants are expected to apply them.

- The profession requires members to conduct themselves and provide services to the public according to certain standards. By upholding these standards, the profession's reputation and standing is protected.

- An accountant's ethical behaviour serves to protect the public interest.

- Consequences of unethical behaviour include disciplinary action against the accountant by their employer or professional body and adverse effects on jobs, financial viability and business efficacy of their organisation.

- Accountants employed in the public sector have a duty to protect tax-payers' money.

It is not enough just to behave ethically, the **values of society** will change over time. Working in the public interest means that accountants must keep up to date with the expectations of society in order to fulfil their role and build confidence in the profession.

Business ethics

The concept of **business ethics** suggests that businesses are morally responsible for their actions, and should be held accountable for the effects of their actions on people and society. This is true for individual businesses (which should behave ethically towards the employees, customers, suppliers and communities who are affected by them) and for 'business' in general, which has a duty to behave responsibly in the interests of the society of which it is a part.

In *Setting the Tone: Ethical Business Leadership* by Philippa Foster Back (2005, published by the Institute of Business Ethics) the author lists some key business values such as truth, transparency, fairness, responsibility and trust.

Some of these ethical values may be explicit: being defined and included in the organisation's mission statement, set out in ethical codes and guidelines, or taught in employee training programmes. Other values may be part of the **organisation culture**: 'the way we do things around here', the unwritten rules and customs of behaviour that develop over time as people find ways of working together.

A **code of ethics** often focuses on social issues. It may set out general principles about an organisation's beliefs on matters such as mission, quality, privacy or the environment. The effectiveness of such codes of ethics depends on the extent to which management supports them 'from the top'. The code of ethics often gives rise to a **code of conduct** for employees.

Task 1

Think of some examples of the kinds of behaviour that you consider 'right' or 'wrong' in your personal and professional life.

THE ROLE OF AN ACCOUNTANT

Before we look at **professional ethics** in detail it is important to consider the role of an accountant, and in particular how ethical dilemmas may arise.

Accountants are generally employed in **three main areas**; in practice, in a business or in the public sector.

Accountants in practice provide services for a number of clients by undertaking professional activities such as producing accounts and tax returns for an individual or business. They may also work in areas such as audit, insolvency or investment business. Such areas are reserved for those authorised to work in them.

An **accountant who works in business** is employed to perform work for the organisation that employs them. For example, a financial accountant may work on the business' financial statements and a management accountant may produce monthly management accounts or other reports used by the senior management team. Those working in business are not usually authorised to perform audit, insolvency or investment work.

Accountants employed in the **public sector** perform similar roles to those employed in business. However, the difference is that their employer is a public service organisation, such as the health service or local government.

It is important to appreciate the wide **variety of work** performed by accountants and how this may put them at risk of different ethical dilemmas depending on their situation.

For example, an **accountant in practice** may have a **conflict of interest** where the interests of two clients clash. An **accountant working in business** or **public sector** won't be at risk of that situation, but could be at risk of **bribes** or **undue influence** from suppliers or other parties interested in their work.

Task 2

Think about the following situations. Do you think the person concerned is acting ethically?

(a)   Somebody who claims unemployment benefit from the state, but who also works part-time, as they cannot otherwise afford to feed their children.

(b)   An airline pilot who decides to risk an emergency landing in severe bad weather for a passenger who is gravely ill and will die if not treated very soon.

(c)   A lottery winner who decides to keep all the winnings for themselves and not to share it with their family.

WHY BEHAVE ETHICALLY?

The AAT has a **Code of Professional Ethics** (the AAT Code) in place, and the most recent revision of it came into force on 1 January 2014. The AAT Code is based on the **Code of Ethics for Professional Accountants** produced by the International Ethics Standards Board for Accountants (IESBA) of the International Federation of Accountants (IFAC). AAT is an full member of IFAC.

The **purpose of the Code** is set out in the foreword. It states that "the decisions you make in the everyday course of your professional lives can have real ethical implications. This is where the code helps. It:

- Sets out the required standards of professional behaviour with guidance to help you achieve them.

- Helps you to protect the public interest.

- Helps you to maintain AAT's good reputation.

IMPORTANT!

This text takes **AAT's Code of Professional Ethics** as an **example** of an **ethical code for accountants**. Your assessment will not refer specifically to the detail of the AAT Code, so you should just focus on the principles of ethical behaviour that it illustrates.

The **ethical code** is in three parts:

- Part A 'General application of the code' applies to all professional accountants.

- Part B represents additional guidance which applies specifically to professional accountants in practice.

- Part C applies specifically to professional accountants in business.

The code has the aim of **identifying the responsibilities** that a person employed as an accountant takes on, in return for a traditionally well paid career with high status. The code identifies potential situations where pitfalls may exist and offers advice on how to deal with them. By doing this the code indicates a minimum level of conduct that all accountants must adhere to.

The **objectives of the accountancy profession** are set out in the ethical code as follows:

(i) The mastering of **particular skills and techniques** acquired through learning and education and maintained through continuing professional development.

(ii) Development of an **ethical approach to work**, as well as to employers and clients. This is acquired by experience and professional supervision under training and is safeguarded by strict ethical and disciplinary codes.

(iii) Acknowledgement of **duties to society** as a whole, in addition to duties to the employer or the client.

(iv) An outlook which is essentially **objective**, obtained by being fair minded and free from conflicts of interest.

(v) Rendering services to the **highest standards** of conduct and performance.

(vi) Achieving **acceptance by the public** that members provide accountancy services in accordance with these high standards and requirements.

The aim of the **ethical code for accountants** is to help professional accountants achieve the above objectives.

There are several **key reasons** why an accountant should strive to behave ethically:

- Ethical issues may be a matter of **law and regulation**. You are expected to know and apply the **civil and criminal law** of the country in which you live and work – as a basic minimum requirement for good practice. The AAT Code for instance is based on the laws effective in the UK, with which AAT members are expected to comply as a minimum requirement. (It is sometimes said that 'the law is a floor': the lowest acceptable level of behaviour required to preserve the public interest and individual rights.)

- Professional accountancy bodies require their members to conduct themselves, and provide services to clients, according to certain professional and ethical standards. They do this, in part, to maintain their own **reputation and standing** – but this is also of benefit to their members and to the accounting profession as a whole.

- Professional and ethical behaviour protects the **public interest**. The accountancy profession has duties to society as a whole – in addition to its specific obligations to employers and clients.

In a nutshell, to behave ethically a **professional accountant** should:

- Completely avoid even the appearance of **conflict of interest** (such as where a personal interest of yours clashes with that of your employer or client).

- Be **objective** and act in the **public interest,** because your responsibility is not exclusively to satisfy the needs of an individual client or employer.

- Keep sensitive information **confidential**. Accountants often deal with their employer's or client's most private material.

- Be **straightforward and honest** in professional and business relationships.

- Maintain **professional knowledge, behaviour and skills** at the level required by a client or employer.

- Act within the **spirit and the letter of the law** so as not to bring the profession into disrepute.

FUNDAMENTAL ETHICAL PRINCIPLES

You might have your own ideas about what 'ethical behaviour' looks like – and these ideas will be shaped by your personal assumptions and values, and the values of the culture in which you operate (at work and in the country in which you live). However, there are five **fundamental principles** set out in the ethical code that underpin ethical behaviour in an accounting context:

Fundamental principle	Explanation	Reference to Part A of AAT Code
Integrity	A member shall be straightforward and honest in all professional and business relationships.	110
Objectivity	A member shall not allow bias, conflict of interest or undue influence of others to override professional or business judgements.	120
Professional competence and due care	A member has a continuing duty to maintain professional knowledge and skill at the level required to ensure that a client or employer receives competent professional service based on current developments in practice, legislation and techniques. A member shall act diligently and in accordance with applicable and professional standards when providing professional services.	130
Confidentiality	A member shall, in accordance with the law, respect the confidentiality of information acquired as a result of professional and business relationships and not disclose any such information to third parties without proper and specific authority unless there is a legal or professional right or duty to disclose. Confidential information acquired as a result of professional and business relationships shall not be used for the personal advantage of the member or third parties.	140
Professional behaviour	A member shall comply with relevant laws and regulations and avoid any action that brings the profession into disrepute.	150

Let's look at each of these in turn.

Integrity

110.1 'The principle of **integrity** imposes an obligation on all members to be straightforward and honest in professional and business relationships. Integrity also implies fair dealing and truthfulness.

110.2 A member shall not be associated with reports, returns, communications or other information where they believe that the information:

(i) Contains a false or misleading statement

(ii) Contains statements or information furnished recklessly

(iii) Omits or obscures information required to be included where such omission or obscurity would be misleading.'

On an everyday level, integrity involves matters such as being **open** about the limitations of your knowledge or competence, being **honest** in your relationships and carrying out your work **accurately, conscientiously and efficiently**. It also means that you should avoid being associated with potentially **misleading information**. It is important therefore to take great care to present your work accurately and in a manner which is, as far as possible, not subject to misinterpretation.

Objectivity

120.1 'The principle of objectivity imposes an obligation on all members not to compromise their professional or business judgement because of bias, conflict of interest or the undue influence of others.'

This is a very important principle for the accounting profession because it protects the interests both of the parties directly affected by an **accountant's services** and of the general public (who rely on the accuracy of information and the integrity of financial systems). Objectivity is the principle that all professional and business judgements should be made fairly:

- On the basis of an **independent** and intellectually honest appraisal of information

- **Free from** all forms of **prejudice** and **bias**

- Free from factors which might affect **impartiality**, such as pressure from a superior, financial interest in the outcome, a personal or professional relationship with one of the parties involved, or a conflict of interest.

Task 3

A member who is straightforward and honest in all business and professional relationships can be said to be following the fundamental principle of objectivity.

	✓
True	
False	

Professional competence and due care

Accountants have an obligation to their employers and clients to know what they are doing – and to do it right! The following is taken from the AAT Code:

130.1 'The principle of **professional competence and due care** imposes the following obligations on members:

  (i) To maintain **professional knowledge** and **skill** at the level required to ensure that clients or employers receive competent professional service and

  (ii) To **act diligently** in accordance with applicable technical and professional standards when providing professional services.

130.2 Competent professional service requires the exercise of **sound judgement** in applying professional knowledge and skill in the performance of such service. Professional competence may be divided into two separate phases:

  (i) Attainment of professional competence and

  (ii) Maintenance of professional competence.

130.3 The **maintenance of professional competence** requires continuing awareness and understanding of relevant technical, professional and business developments. Continuing professional development (CPD) develops and maintains the capabilities that enable a member to perform competently within the professional environment.

130.4 **Diligence** encompasses the **responsibility** to act in accordance with the requirements of an assignment, carefully, thoroughly and on a timely basis.

130.5 A member shall take reasonable steps to ensure that those working under the member's authority in a **professional capacity** have appropriate **training** and **supervision**.

130.6 Where appropriate, a member shall make clients, employers or other users of the professional services aware of **limitations** inherent in the services to avoid the misinterpretation of an expression of opinion as an assertion of fact.'

You should understand from this that you must not agree to carry out a task or assignment if you do not have the competence to carry it out to a **satisfactory standard** – unless you are sure that you will be able to get the help and advice you need to do so. And if you discover in the course of performing a task or assignment that you lack the knowledge or competence to complete it satisfactorily, you should not continue without taking steps to get the help you need.

In addition, once you have become a member of the profession, you need to maintain and develop your professional and **technical competence**, to keep pace with the demands which may be made on you in your work – and developments which may affect your work over time. This may mean:

- **Regularly reviewing** your practices against national and international standards, codes, regulations and legislation. Are you complying with the latest requirements?

- **Continually upgrading** your knowledge and skills in line with developments in accounting practices, requirements and techniques – and making sure that you do not get 'rusty' in the skills you have!

- **Identifying opportunities** to update your knowledge of codes of practice, regulation and legislation. It is important to be proactive in keeping your technical skills up-to-date rather than waiting to be told about changes to matters that affect you.

Task 4

Identify the appropriate word to use in the following sentence:

'Continuing professional development (CPD) is important to accountancy professionals as it helps them [▼] competency in their role.'

Picklist:

attain
maintain

Due care is a concept that means that you should take the degree of care expected of a reasonable person in your position. For example, having agreed to do a task or assignment, you have an obligation to carry it out to the best of your ability, in the client's or employer's best interests, within reasonable timescales and with proper regard for the technical and professional standards expected of you as a professional. As the expert in your field, you may often deal with others who have little knowledge of accounting matters.

This puts you in a position of power, which must never be abused by carrying out your task or assignment in a **negligent** or 'careless' way.

Confidentiality

It is important to note that accountants have a legal duty of confidentiality, as well as the ethical one described below by the AAT Code.

140.1 'The principle of **confidentiality** imposes an obligation on members to refrain from:

    (i) **Disclosing** outside the firm or employing organisation confidential information acquired as a result of professional and business relationships without proper and specific authority or unless there is a legal or professional right or duty to disclose and

    (ii) **Using confidential information** acquired as a result of professional and business relationships to their personal advantage or the advantage of third parties.

    Information about a past, present, or prospective client's or **employer's affairs**, or the affairs of clients of employers, acquired in a work context, is likely to be confidential if it is not a matter of public knowledge.

140.2 A member shall maintain confidentiality even in a **social environment**. The member shall be alert to the possibility of inadvertent disclosure, particularly in circumstances involving close or personal relations, associates and long established business relationships.

140.3 A member shall maintain confidentiality of information disclosed by a **prospective client** or **employer**.

140.4 A member shall maintain confidentiality of information within the firm or **employing organisation**.

140.5 A member shall take all **reasonable steps** to ensure that **staff under their control** and persons from whom advice and assistance is obtained **respect** the principle of **confidentiality**. The restriction on using confidential information also means not using it for any purpose other than that for which it was legitimately acquired.

140.6 The need to comply with the principle of confidentiality **continues even after the end of relationships** between a member and a client or employer. When a member changes employment or acquires a new client, the member is entitled to use prior experience. The member shall not, however, use or disclose any confidential information either acquired or received as a result of a professional or business relationship.'

Confidentiality is a very important fundamental principle but there are circumstances where the law **allows or requires** that confidentiality to be breached.

These circumstances are described in the AAT Code in section 140.7 and are summarised in the following table.

Circumstance	Examples
Disclosure is permitted by law and is authorised by the client or employer.	Providing working papers to a new firm who is taking on the client.
Disclosure is required by law.	Providing documents or other evidence for legal proceedings.
	Disclosure to the authorities, such as Her Majesty's Revenue and Customs (HMRC) in relation to taxation matters.
	Disclosure of actual/suspected money laundering or terrorist financing to the firm's Money Laundering Reporting Officer (MLRO) or to the National Crime Agency (NCA) (in the UK). We shall look at money laundering in Chapter 4.
There is a professional right or duty to disclose which is in the public interest and is not prohibited by law.	Complying with the quality review of an IFAC member body or other professional body.
	Responding to an inquiry or investigation by the AAT or other regulatory or professional body.
	Disclosure to protect the member's professional interests in legal proceedings.
	A disclosure made to comply with technical standards and ethics requirements.

It is vital to appreciate the importance of the fundamental principle of **confidentiality**. You need to respect the confidentiality of information acquired as a result of professional and business relationships. This means that you will not use or disclose confidential information to others, or use it for your own benefit, unless:

- You have **specific** and **'proper' authorisation** to do so by the client or employer.

- You are legally or professionally **entitled** or **obliged** to do so.

It is also worth being aware that personal information shared with you by clients and colleagues at work should be regarded as confidential – unless you are told otherwise. This is an important basis for **trust** in any working relationship.

Trust links us back to **personal** and **professional ethics** that we saw at the start of this chapter and you should also keep it in mind as we continue our look at professional behaviour.

Task 5

In which of the following circumstances do you have a legal duty to disclose confidential information concerning a customer of your organisation?

	✓
If they are asked for during legal proceedings.	
When your manager tells you to disclose the information.	
When writing a report for general circulation within your organisation.	

Professional behaviour

The final fundamental principle is professional behaviour. On this principle the AAT Code states:

> 150.1 The principle of **professional behaviour** imposes an obligation on members to comply with relevant laws and regulations and avoid any action that may bring disrepute to the profession. This includes actions which a **reasonable and informed third party**, having knowledge of all relevant information, would conclude negatively affect the good reputation of the profession.
>
> Members should note that conduct reflecting adversely on the reputation of the AAT is a ground for disciplinary action under the AAT's *Disciplinary Regulations*.'

An example of the principle is given in section 150.2 of the AAT Code which highlights that accountants in practice must be honest and truthful when advertising their services. They can bring the profession into disrepute by making **exaggerated claims** about services, their qualifications and experience, or if they make **disparaging references or unsubstantiated comparisons** to the work of others.

Applying this principle means **'being professional'**. You'll have your own ideas about what 'being professional' means, but fundamentally it involves:

- Complying with the law – the 'law is the floor', and

- Behaving in a way that maintains or enhances the reputation of your profession: bringing it credit – not discredit.

One key aspect of this is **courtesy**. As a professional, you should behave with courtesy and consideration towards anyone you come into contact with in the course of your work and indeed in your personal life.

> **It is IMPOSSIBLE for us to overstate the importance of each of these fundamental principles – you MUST be able to recognise each of them.**

HOW IT WORKS

Now that we've considered the fundamental principles in general, let's consider some typical scenarios in which they might be helpful. In each case, we will identify the ethical issues they present, in line with the basic principles discussed so far, and make some 'common sense' suggestions for what you should do about it. For the purposes of these questions you should assume you are an AAT student.

Incident one

You are asked to produce an aged receivables' listing for your manager as soon as possible. However you do not have up to date figures because of a problem with the computer system. A colleague suggests that to get the report done in time you use averages for the missing figures.

There is an **integrity** issue here. Using averages instead of actual figures will almost certainly result in an inaccurate listing. You should report the problem to your manager and ask for an extension to your deadline in order to provide an accurate listing.

Incident two

You have received a letter from an estate agent, requesting financial information about one of your company's customers that is applying to rent a property. The information is needed as soon as possible, by fax or email, in order to secure approval for the rent agreement.

There is a **confidentiality** issue here. You need the customer's authority to disclose the information; you may also need to confirm the identity of the person making the request. You should also take steps to protect the confidentiality of the information when you send it: for example, not using fax or email (which can be intercepted), and stating clearly that the information is confidential.

Incident three

While out to lunch, you run into a friend at the sandwich bar. In conversation, she tells you that she expects to inherit some money from a recently deceased uncle, and asks you how she will be affected by inheritance tax, capital gains tax and other matters.

There are issues of **professional competence and due care** here. You are not qualified to give advice on matters of taxation. Even if you were qualified, any answer you give on the spot would risk being incomplete or inaccurate with potentially serious consequences.

Incident four

A client of the accountancy practice you work in is so pleased with the service you gave him this year that he offers you a free weekend break in a luxury hotel, just as a 'thank you'.

There is an **objectivity** issue here as the gift is of significant value. Think about how it looks: a third party observer is entitled to wonder what 'special favours' deserve this extra reward – and/or how such a gift may bias you in the client's favour in future.

THE CONCEPTUAL FRAMEWORK

It is impossible to give guidelines on every possible situation that may arise in the course of your work which conflicts with the fundamental ethical principles. The ethical code for accountants therefore sets out a basic **problem solving procedure**, which you can use in any situation, to give yourself the best chance of complying with the principles. This procedure forms the '**conceptual framework**' which requires the following:

- Identify where there may be a **threat** to a fundamental principle.

- **Evaluate the threat**: how significant is it?

- For any significant threat **apply safeguards** that will eliminate the threat or reduce it to an acceptable level (so that compliance with the fundamental principle is not compromised).

- If safeguards cannot be applied, **decline or discontinue** the specific action or professional service involved, or where necessary, **resign** from the client (if you are a member in practice) or the employing organisation (if you are a member in business).

Identifying and evaluating threats and the application of safeguards all require the application of an accountant's **professional judgement.**

Although professional judgement is a **personal view**, based on an accountant's training and experience, it is expected that members of the profession would act in a broadly similar way given the same circumstances.

We shall now look at threats and safeguards in more detail.

Threats

Many of the threats that may create a risk of compromising the fundamental principles will fall into one of the following five categories.

Threat	Explanation	Examples
Self-interest	Financial or other interests may inappropriately influence the member's judgement or behaviour	Undue fee dependence on one particular client by an accountant in practice
Self-review	A previous judgement needs to be re-evaluated by the member responsible for that judgement	Tax and accountancy work carried out by the same engagement team
Advocacy	A member promotes a position or opinion to the point that subsequent objectivity may be compromised	Acting on behalf of an assurance client which is in litigation or dispute with a third party
Familiarity	Due to close or personal relationships, a member becomes too sympathetic to the interests of others	A senior member undertaking an assurance engagement for a number of years for the same client
Intimidation	A member may be deterred from acting objectively by threats (actual or perceived)	Threatened withdrawal of services by a dominant client

It is important to note that not all threats are capable of being categorised in this way. If you come across such a threat, it is important not to ignore it, but deal with it as best you can.

Safeguards

The AAT Code defines safeguards as '**actions or other measures that may eliminate threats or reduce them to an acceptable level.**' This basically means that a safeguard is something you can do when you encounter a threat.

The Code identifies two broad categories of safeguards that you might use to reduce or eliminate the threats we have described above.

- **Safeguards created by the profession and/or legislation and regulation.** These include:

    - Education, training and experience, as requirements for entry into the profession

    - Continuing professional development (CPD)

    - Corporate governance regulations

    - Professional standards

    - Professional or regulatory monitoring and disciplinary procedures

    - External review of financial reports, returns, communications or information produced by members

- **Safeguards in the work environment**, which increase the likelihood of identifying or deterring unethical behaviour, include:

    - Quality controls, and internal audits of quality controls

    - Mechanisms to empower and protect staff who raise ethical concerns ('whistleblowers')

    - Involvement of, or consultation with, independent third parties (eg non executive directors or regulatory bodies)

    - Rotation of personnel to avoid increasing familiarity and opportunities for collusion in fraud

    - Opportunities to discuss ethical dilemmas (eg with an ethics officer, committee or forum)

Specific safeguards are considered in more detail in later chapters in terms of members in practice and members in business.

Task 6

Jake has been put under significant pressure by his manager to change the conclusion of a report he has written which reflects badly on the manager's performance. Which threat is Jake facing?

	✓
Self-interest	
Advocacy	
Intimidation	

PRINCIPLES VERSUS RULES

The accountancy profession could have a taken a **rules-based approach** to ethics. This would have involved creating a large book of rules trying to cover every possible ethical scenario that could be faced, with an answer to every single ethical problem. Instead, the ethical code is based on fundamental principles, which you should apply in all your work. By contrast the approach to ethical requirements in the US is largely rules-based.

This **principles-based approach** to ethics encourages a case-by-case deliberation, judgement and responsibility that can be applied to the infinite variety of circumstances that arise in the modern business environment. Hopefully, this will encourage a more flexible approach to ethical problems, whilst at the same time promoting ethical awareness. This approach is advocated by the IESBA *Code of Ethics for Professional Accountants* on which the AAT, along with many other professional bodies in the accountancy profession, bases its ethical code.

Consider the pros and cons of the principles- and rules-based approaches:

Rules-based approach – advantages

- Rules are clear-cut, leaving no room for misunderstanding.
- The correct course of action is likely to be obvious.
- Rules-based approaches are easier to enforce.

Rules-based approach – disadvantages

- You can wriggle out of your obligations by finding loopholes; it is often said that rules encourage avoidance.

- Promotes a 'tick box' mentality, with concern for the letter of the rule, rather than its spirit.

- Must legislate for every circumstance, necessitating a large number of detailed requirements.

- New requirements must be developed as circumstances change.

- There is a risk of getting swamped by the details and missing the big picture.

Principles-based approach – advantages

- Sets more rigorous standards of behaviour as you must comply with the spirit, not just the letter, of the requirements. It is often said that principles encourage compliance.

- Helps you see the bigger picture rather than just individual rules.

- Flexible – can keep up with a rapidly changing business environment and be applied in differing circumstances across the world.

- Develops ethical judgement and decision-making skills.

- Helps create a culture of ethical awareness.

- Encourages you to take responsibility for your actions.

Principles-based approach – disadvantages

- It is not always easy to find the right answer or even to identify the right questions.

- There may be more than one correct course of action and conflicting interests and priorities must be carefully balanced.

COMPLIANCE WITH THE LAW

All individuals and organisations are expected to accept and obey the law, rather than to break it. As we saw earlier, the **law is a floor** – in other words it is the minimum level of behaviour expected by society and is a base from which ethics and professional rules of behaviour are built on. In the UK, law falls into two categories:

- **Criminal law – offences** relating to persons or property that affect the whole community. Punishment for a breach of criminal law (for the crimes of theft, money laundering, terrorist financing, bribery or fraud, for example) is most likely to result in fines or imprisonment imposed by the state. Where an individual is taken to court for committing a criminal offence, they are said to be **prosecuted** in a criminal court.

- **Civil law – wrongs** relating to conflicts between individuals and organisations within the community. There is no involvement of the state. Civil law conflicts (known as lawsuits), may be for breach of contract, negligence and trust, for example, and the remedies awarded are designed to place the injured party in the position they would have been in if the breach had not occurred. The concept of punishment does not apply. Civil cases are **heard** in a civil court.

Accountants are affected by a range of laws which they should be aware of. Some laws are created by the **Government** and are known as **legislation** or **statute law.** Other laws are created by the decisions of **Judges** when they hear civil and criminal cases brought before them. These laws are known as **common law** and they build-up over time as case after case are heard.

Some laws are not necessarily obvious such as **health and safety legislation,** and **employment protection and equality laws**.

- Members who are employees have duties under health and safety legislation to take precautions against risk of injury and to report potential risks to management. Members who are self employed have duties to protect the health and safety of their employees.

- All employees have a general duty to behave in ways that contribute to, and maintain, a healthy and safe workplace. Reckless behaviour endangers both yourself and others: creating the risk of accidents, fire, security breach and so on.

- Employment protection and equality laws concern rules on whether an employer can dismiss employees without being liable for claims for wrongful and unfair dismissal. It also includes legislation in the UK on treating employees fairly, for example without discriminating against them due to their age, sex, religion or sexual orientation.

When deciding whether or not behaviour is ethical, compliance with the law is assumed as a starting point: 'the law is a floor'. The Introduction to the AAT Code states that:

> 1.8 'The code is based on the laws effective in the UK, **which members are expected to comply with as a minimum requirement.** Members working or living overseas are expected to know and apply the laws of the overseas country, having taken local legal advice if necessary. Where this code refers to legal issues, it does not purport to give definitive legal advice or to cover every situation, nor does this code highlight every legal issue that members may need to consider. Members who encounter problems in relation to legal aspects are recommended to seek their own legal advice.'

The key point to remember about the AAT's Code is that it is **not legally enforceable**. It provides a set of guidelines set by the profession and failing to meet them will **not** result in a member breaking the civil or criminal law. Any penalties are at the discretion of the AAT and subject to the member's conduct adversely reflecting on the reputation of the AAT. The Code contrasts with **laws** (such as contract law), which are legally enforceable, and those who breach it will face the legal consequences.

The AAT's Code does have **limits** as members are also subject to legal or other regulations depending on the work they do.

For example accountants that work in the reserved areas of audit, insolvency or investment must comply with rules set by the regulatory bodies, and accountants in business must comply with regulations in their industrial sector. There are also some rules that everyone must comply with, such as health and safety and employment law legislation.

THE ACCOUNTANCY PROFESSION

We set out the objectives of the accountancy profession at the start of this chapter.

In the UK, the accountancy profession is largely **self-regulatory**, with the **professional accountancy bodies** (such as the AAT) each responsible for setting and upholding the ethical standards of their members.

The **senior bodies** of the accountancy profession (see the following diagram) are under the supervision of the Codes and Standards Committee (CSC), and the Conduct Committee (CC) of the **Financial Reporting Council** (FRC) and are regulated by statute on how they govern the professional bodies.

We examine the role of the FRC and its constituent committees below.

The Financial Reporting Council (FRC)

The FRC is the UK's independent regulator for the accountancy and actuarial professions. It was established to promote ethical financial reporting and increased confidence in the accountancy profession, corporate reporting and governance.

The structure of the FRC is shown in the diagram below:

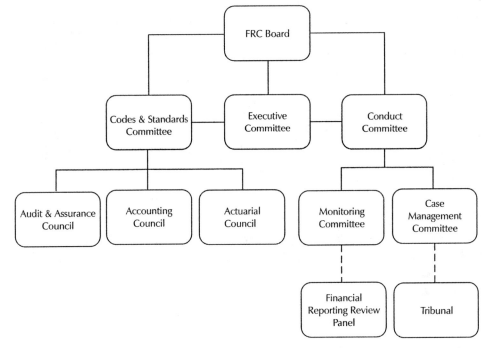

The FRC Board is supported by three committees, the Executive Committee, the Codes and Standards Committee and the Conduct Committee.

The **Executive Committee's role** is to oversee the day-to-day work of the FRC as an organisation and to advise the FRC Board on strategic issues.

The role of the **Codes and Standards Committee** is to develop the UK framework of codes and standards in the areas of accounting, audit and assurance, actuarial, corporate governance and shareholder engagement (stewardship). The Committee is supported by three Councils (the **Audit and Assurance Council**, the **Accounting Council** and the **Actuarial Council**).

Each Council is responsible for developing Codes and Standards relevant to its area of interest, considering relevant international developments (and if necessary responding to them) and advising the FRC Board on any research or other developments within its remit.

The **Conduct Committee** is responsible for the FRC's Conduct Division and it is supported by the **Monitoring Committee** and the **Case Management Committee.**

The **Monitoring Committee** is responsible for: monitoring the professional accountancy bodies that, under legislation, regulate their members involved in audit, insolvency and investment business.

The **major accountancy bodies** that are monitored by the FRC in this way are the chartered accountancy bodies:

- Institute of Chartered Accountants in England and Wales (ICAEW)
- Association of Chartered Certified Accountants (ACCA)
- Institute of Chartered Accountants of Scotland (ICAS)
- Chartered Accountants Ireland (CAI)

You should note that the AAT does not fall under the FRC's monitoring remit.

FRC is also the ultimate disciplinary body for the accountancy profession, – the Case Management Committee having the role of handling disciplinary cases.

Task 7

Which body of the FRC oversees the day-to-day work of the organisation?

	✓
The Executive Committee	
The FRC Board	
The Conduct Committee	

The International Federation of Accountants

Earlier in this chapter, we explained that the ethical code for accountants, of which the AAT Code is exemplar, is essentially the *Code of Ethics for Professional Accountants*, produced by the IESBA which is part of IFAC. Let's look at the role of IFAC in a bit more detail now.

IFAC is an **international body** representing all the **major accountancy bodies** across the world. Its mission is to develop the high standards of professional accountants and enhance the quality of services they provide.

IFAC's mission is to:

- Serve the public interest
- Strengthen the worldwide accountancy profession
- Establish and promote adherence to high quality professional standards
- Promote further international convergence of these standards

To enable the development of high standards IESBA, IFAC's ethics committee, established the **Code of Ethics for Professional Accountants**, which has aligned standards globally. This means that accountants around the world are expected to follow the same set of principles.

BPP
LEARNING MEDIA

The Consultative Committee of Accountancy Bodies (CCAB)

The major chartered accountancy professional bodies in the UK and Ireland joined together in 1974 to form the **Consultative Committee of Accountancy Bodies**. CCAB currently has five members:

- The Institute of Chartered Accountants in England and Wales (ICAEW)
- The Institute of Chartered Accountants of Scotland (ICAS)
- Chartered Accountants Ireland (CAI)
- The Association of Chartered Certified Accountants (ACCA)
- The Chartered Institute of Public Finance and Accountancy (CIPFA)

CCAB provides a forum in which matters affecting the profession can be discussed and co-ordinated, and enables the profession to speak with a unified voice.

The AAT itself is not part of the CCAB, and neither is the Chartered Institute of Management Accountants (CIMA).

The **AAT is a qualification** and **membership body** for accounting staff. The qualifications of the AAT are vocational; members are accountants who have practical accounting skills for use in the workplace. The qualification allows a **vocational progression route** to the UK's chartered accountancy qualifications if desired.

AAT members are **licensed** by the AAT to provide **accounting and tax services**, but as the AAT is not a Recognised Qualifying Body or a Recognised Supervisory Body, members are not permitted to call themselves chartered accountants.

It is worth noting that three of the bodies that make up the CCAB – ICAEW, ICAS, and CIPFA – are **sponsoring bodies** of the AAT. The fourth sponsoring body of the AAT is the Chartered Institute of Management Accountants (CIMA).

A person does not have to be a member of a professional accountancy body to offer services as an accountant in the UK. The term 'accountant' is not protected in law and anyone may call themselves one. Examples of work carried out by accountants who may not be professionally qualified include the provision of bookkeeping and payroll services. However, such 'accountants' must register with **Her Majesty's Revenue and Customs** (HMRC) as a **provider of an accountancy service**. This is because their work is subject to Money Laundering Regulations and must be supervised.

The profession points out that the training and CPD requirements of the accountancy bodies means that **qualified accountants** provide a better service than unqualified accountants. It is also a fact that qualified accountants working in practice are required to hold Professional Indemnity (PI) insurance to protect their clients if something goes wrong. There is no such obligation on those working as unqualified accountants.

In relation to **Money Laundering Regulations**, that we shall look at in Chapter 4, a professional body such as the AAT is classified as a **supervisory body**. This means that the work and behaviour of qualified accountants are subject to supervision by their professional body – an extra degree of assurance for clients and employers.

HM Revenue & Customs (HMRC)

HM Revenue & Customs (HMRC) is a government department that was set up in 2005as a result of the merger of the Inland Revenue and HM Customs and Excise. Its aim is to ensure that the correct tax is paid at the right time.

It collects and administers direct taxes (eg income tax, capital gains tax, corporation tax, inheritance tax and National Insurance) and indirect taxes (eg VAT, stamp duty and excise duties). It pays and administers child benefit, child trust funds and tax credits. It also protects us by enforcing and administering border and frontier protection, environmental taxes, national minimum wage enforcement and recovery of student loans.

National Crime Agency (NCA)

The **National Crime Agency** (NCA) is a non-ministerial Government department. Its aim is to tackle serious organised crime that affects the United Kingdom and its citizens. Serious organised crime includes Class A drugs, human trafficking, fraud, money laundering and terrorist financing. The NCA is accountable to the Home Secretary and ultimately Parliament.

The **NCA** operates through the following **'four pillars'**:

Pursue – to disrupt and prosecute individuals who undertake serious and organised crime.

Prevent – to prevent individuals from taking part in serious and organised crime.

Protect – to protect the public against serious and organised crime.

Prepare – to lessen the impact of serious and organised crime.

In relation to this text, you need to know about the role of NCA in countering money laundering and terrorist financing, which we discuss in detail in later chapters.

CODES OF CONDUCT AND CODES OF PRACTICE

When considering ensuring ethical behaviour, **codes of conduct** and **codes of practice** are often mentioned. Although the terms are often used interchangeably, there are in fact subtle differences between them.

Code of conduct (employee ethics)

A **code of conduct** is designed to influence the behaviour of employees: it sets out the procedures to be used in specific ethical situations – such as conflicts of interest or the acceptance of gifts, and the procedures to determine whether a violation occurred and what remedies should be imposed. The effectiveness of such codes depends on the extent to which management supports them. **Violations** of a code of conduct, or **other types of misconduct**, may make the violator subject to the organisation's disciplinary procedures which could even result in them losing their job.

Code of practice (professional ethics)

A **code of practice** is adopted by a profession or organisation to regulate its members, and provide clear guidance on what behaviour is considered ethical and appropriate, in terms of good practice, in the circumstances. In a membership context, failure to comply with a code of practice can result in disciplinary action by the professional organisation. The ethical code for accountants is an example of a code of practice.

Codes of conduct and practice often have a special legal status. They are **not legally binding** on employees and members – only legislation can do that. But if a company is being prosecuted, for example for breaking health and safety law, and it can be shown that its organisation's code of practice was not followed, then the court may be more likely to find the company at fault. However, the actual outcome will depend entirely on the circumstances.

Industry sector codes

Many **industries** introduce their own codes of conduct and practice to regulate the activities of member businesses and individuals. **Industry codes** are often **voluntary**, but some have a **statutory basis** and are legally binding.

Example:

The UK's Advertising Standards Authority (ASA) is the self-regulatory organisation for the advertising industry. Its rules do not have a statutory basis and it has no power to enforce legislation, but its code does broadly reflect the requirements of relevant legislation and in that way it attempts to keep its members from acting unlawfully.

BUSINESS ETHICS AND PROFESSIONAL VALUES

The concept of **business ethics** suggests that businesses are morally responsible for their actions, and should be held accountable for the effects of their actions on people and society.

This is true for individual businesses and for 'business' in general, which has a duty to behave responsibly in the interests of the society of which it is a part.

The importance of business values in a company's culture is that they underpin both policy and behaviour throughout the company, from top to bottom.

Managers usually have a duty to aim for profit. At the same time, ethical standards require them to protect the rights of a range of groups inside and outside the organisation who have a legitimate interest or 'stake' in the organisation's activities. These groups are often known as **stakeholders**.

Business ethics are also relevant to **competitive behaviour**: there is a distinction between competing aggressively and competing unethically (for example, by stealing competitors' designs; using buyer power to prevent suppliers from dealing with competitors; or spreading false negative information about competitors).

A consequence of the need for a business to act ethically is for it to **change its culture** so all employees, managers and directors know what is expected of them. For example, management might 'turn a blind eye' to employees submitting inflated expense claims, but this is not something an ethical organisation would allow, so the attitude of employees and mangers must be changed so that only accurate expense claims are made

Effective ethical programmes and codes of conduct

There are three elements to creating an effective ethical programme for a business:

Active leadership (setting the 'tone at the top')

The programme, and the ethical corporate culture that it aims to develop, should be supported by the very top of the organisation. A senior board member should be appointed as 'Ethical Champion', whose initial role is to persuade all other senior executives to lead by example.

Buy-in

The Champion's next role is to organise a consultation process with members of staff to achieve their 'buy-in' to the new ethical culture. All staff should understand that the ethical code gives them principles and values that should be reflected in their everyday activities, and will help them deal with any ethical issues they come across while at work.

Training

Once employees understand the need for ethical behaviour and embrace the change in culture, training should be provided to ensure that all understand what is expected of them, and to further instil the ethical message. Helplines may be set up to provide employees with advice for dealing with ethical problems.

Benefits of a code of conduct

Organisations that develop and introduce codes of conduct find a number of benefits from doing so, which include:

Communication

Ethical codes communicate the standard of behaviour expected of employees and help them make the right choice between alternative courses of action.

Consistency of conduct

With the ethical message effectively communicated, the behaviour of employees can be standardised or made consistent across all operations and locations. Customers, suppliers and other stakeholders will receive similar treatment wherever they are.

Risk reduction

Standardised behaviour reduces the risk of unethical actions, as employees who are unethical will 'stand out' and can be dealt with. This reduces the risk of a few employees irrevocably damaging the reputation of the organisation and the trust people have in it.

The Nolan Principles of Public Life

The Committee on Standards in Public Life is an advisory body of the UK government which was established in response to concerns that conduct by some politicians was unethical. The **Nolan Committee** report established **The Seven Principles of Public Life**. These principles are relevant in part to accountants due to some similarities with the fundamental principles set out in the ethical Code.

The **key principles** include:

Integrity

Individuals should not place themselves under any financial or other obligation to third parties that might seek to influence them in the performance of their duties.

Objectivity

When making decisions, such as awarding contracts or recommending others for promotion, an individual should make their choice on merit.

Accountability

Individuals are personally accountable for their decisions and actions and must submit themselves to whatever scrutiny is appropriate.

Openness

Individuals should open about all the decisions and actions that they take. They should give reasons for their decisions and restrict information only when the wider interest clearly demands.

Honesty

Individuals have a duty to declare any private interests relating to their duties and to take steps to resolve any conflicts arising in a way that protects the wider interest.

SUSTAINABILITY AND CORPORATE SOCIAL RESPONSIBILITY

We saw earlier that accountants are expected to act in and protect the **public interest**, and in the modern business world, the concepts of **sustainability** and **corporate social responsibility** are increasingly important in this regard.

Sustainability

The **key definition of sustainability** can be found in the **UN's Brundtland Report**. According to this, organisations must aim to 'meet the needs of the present without compromising the ability of future generations to meet their own needs.'

Sustainable development is a core part of an organisation's corporate social responsibility (see below). It means that an organisation should develop its operations in such a way as to co-exist with society, rather than compete with it, in order for both to have a future. In other words, it should put the long-term future ahead of short-term gains.

Corporate social responsibility

The concept of corporate social responsibility (CSR) was established by the expectation in society that **companies are accountable** for the social and ethical effects of their actions.

A company's CSR can be defined as the **obligations** that it feels that it has to its, local community, persons and organisations connected to it and to society as a whole. For example, organisations that source materials from developing countries may feel they should pay a fair price for the goods they buy, rather than the minimum they can get away with. As accountants play a **central role** in the operation of a business, they are key to the organisation upholding these values.

DUTIES AND RESPONSIBILITIES OF FINANCE PROFESSIONALS IN RELATION TO SUSTAINABILITY

The definition of sustainability from the **UN's Brundtland Report** makes it clear that business organisations have a duty to **protect society** and **future generations**, and as part of the business world, finance professionals have a duty to consider the **economic (financial)**, **social** and **environmental** aspects of their work in order to support sustainability. This duty is in additional to the general public interest duty that we have already seen that accountants have.

Duties of finance professionals

The **economic (financial)**, **social** and **environmental issues** mentioned above are collectively known as the **'triple bottom line'** and should be considered by accountants in all the work that they do.

Economic (financial) aspects include an accountant supporting their organisation or clients to be profitable, supporting local businesses when deciding on suppliers and paying them on time, building long-term relationships with suppliers and clients, and looking for ways to improve the efficiency of the organisation's finance operations.

Social aspects are fair and beneficial business practices towards labour, the community and region in which an organisation conducts its business. These practices are aimed at ensuring the well-being of the organisation, its workforce and other stakeholders as their interests are interdependent. An example of such a practice would be a policy on consulting the local community when the organisation is making a decision on investing in or relocating operations.

Environmental aspects are usually in relation to using less energy and creating less pollution. An accountant should therefore support company policies on the long-term management of resources and facilitating the running of their organisation in a sustainable manner. These may include, for example, not printing emails unless necessary, turning lights off at the end of the day and recycling materials used in their office.

Risks of not acting sustainably

There are a **number of risks** to the **organisation** and **society** of **not acting sustainably**. As resources are used up and get more scarce, their price will rise and so will the manufacturing organisation's costs. Acting sustainably now may prevent or delay such price rises. The government may legislate to prevent or reduce the depletion of resources, and such legislation may be more stringent and restrictive than if businesses voluntarily change their practices.

For society, the lack of sustainability now may mean fewer products in the future as the resources used to make them are used up. Damage to the environment due to pollution may become irreversible and lead to long-term changes to the planet. Ultimately the cost of goods will rise due to the rise in price of the resources used to make them.

Responsibilities of finance professionals

There are six main responsibilities of finance professionals in regards to upholding the principles of sustainability.

Creating and promoting an ethics-based culture

A culture is often defined by the phrase 'the way we do things around here'. Essentially it means the shared values, ways of working and history that define the organisation. Finance professionals should help senior management create and promote an ethics-based culture within their organisation. Primarily it means supporting ethical policies as they are introduced, but it also means discouraging illegal or unethical practices if they are aware of them. Such practices may include, for example, money laundering, terrorist financing, fraud, theft, bribery, non-compliance with regulations, bullying and short-term decision making.

Championing the aims of sustainability

The aims of sustainability, as identified by the UN's Brundtland Report, should be promoted and followed. However, the finance professional should remain objective at all times. This means that the aims should not be followed blindly, but instead be followed within the context of the organisation's culture and its own policies on sustainability.

Evaluating and quantifying reputational and other ethical risks

Finance professionals prepare and present information used by senior managers in their decision making and risk analysis. To be able to perform this work to a high level, they often have well-developed analysis and evaluation skills. This means they are among the best placed within an organisation to deal with reputational and other risks. We shall consider these risks in detail shortly.

Taking social, environmental and financial factors into account

Social, environmental and financial factors are together known as the 'triple bottom line'. Many organisations demonstrate their commitment to corporate social responsibility (CSR) by including, in their financial reports, organisational performance information based on these factors. Historically, financial professionals have focussed on the financial bottom line, but now they have a responsibility to take social and environmental factors into account as well. This means that when organisational position and performance is measured, the business can clearly demonstrate its commitment to CSR.

Promoting sustainable practices

As well as promoting policies in relation to ethical and illegal practices, finance professionals should also support sustainability practices developed by the organisation. Such **practices** may be in relation to the following areas:

- Products and services (minimise waste in the actual product or service)
- Customers (make the products easy for the customer to recycle)
- Employees (employ local staff)
- Workplace (energy efficient lighting and good insulation)
- Suppliers (use local suppliers)
- Business functions and processes (minimise pollution in production)

Raising awareness of social responsibility

As mentioned earlier, finance professionals should consider social responsibility and the sustainability impacts of their decisions and actions. By doing so, they will help raise awareness within the organisation as colleagues, who may be in different departments, see them taking a lead in this area.

Task 8

Think of some examples of sustainability and corporate social responsibility issues in the place that you work.

RISKS FROM IMPROPER PRACTICE

We have already come across risk in earlier parts of this chapter, for example the risk of an accountant breaching their ethical principles and the risk of a business breaching health and safety legislation. These are important risks that accountants and business organisations should consider, however it is possible to **classify the various risks** into broad categories. By categorising risks in this way, we are able to analyse and manage them.

Risk can be **defined** as the possibility of loss or damage caused by factors inside or outside the organisation that may be avoided by taking pre-emptive action. Business risk can be further broken down into the following categories.

Operational risk

A particularly important risk is **operational risk**. This may be defined as the chance of loss or damage to the organisation that is caused by faulty internal processes or personnel, or as a consequence of events that occur outside of it.

An operational risk is therefore the risk of losses arising simply from the day-to-day business of the company – whether through its processes, its staff, its systems or from external events.

It is a broad concept including, but not limited to, the risk of fraud, legal risks, physical and environmental risks. Risk management is usually carried out within the various business functions, and so it becomes an issue that affects every member of staff. For example, the IT department will take care of the risks associated with the processing, storage and use of information, and the human resources department will take care of personnel risks through its recruitment and selection procedures.

It is important to understand that some of the factors which contribute to something going wrong in how the organisation conducts its business can be controlled to some extent by codes of conduct and an ethical programme. Therefore there is a link between good ethical safeguards and a reduction in operational risk and associated losses.

Operational risk can be classified into:

- **Reputational risk** – loss or damage to an organisation through loss of its reputation.

- **Litigation risk** – loss or damage which is the consequence of legal action or failure to follow a code of practice.

- **Process risk** – losses resulting from poorly designed business processes.

- **People risk** – losses resulting from human error or deliberate actions.

- **Systems risk** – losses resulting from poorly designed systems such as internal and external controls.

- **Legal risk** – losses resulting from failure to adhere to legal requirements.

- **Event risk** – losses from one-off or on-going incidents such as a fire in a factory or the collapse of a market for the organisation's products.

Examples of operational risk

The following are some specific examples of operational risks. Questions of ethics and ethical behaviour could arise in each one.

- Internal fraud
- External fraud
- Employment practices and workplace safety
- Clients, products and business practice
- Damage to physical assets
- Business disruption and systems failures
- Processes and delivery of outputs

Types of event risk

Event risks may be classified is according to their sources in the env

- **Physical risks**: such as climate and geology, natural disast
- **Social risks**: changes in tastes, attitudes and demography.
- **Political risks**: changes determined by government, or by change of government including changes in legislation and regulations, including the consequences of breaking the law or otherwise failing to meet legal duties or obligations.
- **Economic risks**: changing economic conditions and operating environment including technological changes.

Risk and accountants

All operational risks are real issues for accountants but there are safeguards in place to help reduce them. For example, following the customer due diligence rules required by the money laundering regulations when new clients are taken on will help reduce operational risk related to business practice. These relate specifically to money laundering and we shall look at the details later on.

Risks from unethical behaviour

Unethical behaviour by an organisation's managers and employees creates a number of risks for the organisation that the accountant should be aware of and look out for. Examples of **risks** that **result** from **unethical behaviour** include:

- Damage to company brand and image as a consequence of public awareness of unethical behaviour.
- Reduced levels of employee performance and consequential effect on corporate productivity.
- Increased absenteeism.
- Reduced discipline of employees and generation of conflict between individuals within the organisation.
- Increased employee turnover rates.
- Increased dysfunctional behaviour (such as lack of attention to detail, withholding information, under-delivering and misrepresenting results) with knock-on effect on organisational performance.
- Reduced corporate value.
- Losses due to regulatory fines for non-compliance with rules and regulations.

Task 9

Damage to assets such as vehicles and buildings is an example of a loss resulting from which type of operational risk?

	✓
Reputational	
Litigation	
Physical	

DISCIPLINARY ACTION BY A PROFESSIONAL BODY AND EMPLOYER

We have considered above the risks to an organisation of improper practice. There are also consequences for the **individual accountant** of non-compliance with codes of practice and regulations, and with the ethical code for accountants.

An accountant who is found to have committed **misconduct** by their professional body will face a number of consequences, such as a **fine** or **expulsion** from membership.

Misconduct may be **defined** as, 'conduct by an individual that would, in the opinion of the professional body, prejudice their status as a member or reflect adversely on the reputation of the body'. Therefore an individual that has acted in serious or repeated breach of their body's rules, regulations or bylaws is likely to be found guilty of misconduct.

If an accountant's actions are sufficient for them to be disciplined by their professional body, then it is likely that they may be in breach of their **employer's internal disciplinary rules** as well. If this is the case then they may receive some form of punishment from their employer too. Punishments will depend on the **severity of the behaviour.** Minor issues, such as rude behaviour, may be dealt with by an informal or formal warning not to continue the misconduct. Major breaches of discipline, such as theft, may result in them losing their job.

CONTINUING PROFESSIONAL DEVELOPMENT (CPD)

CPD was mentioned earlier in this chapter when we looked at the fundamental principle of professional competence and due care.

According to the AAT Code: 'CPD develops and maintains the capabilities that enable a member to perform competently within the professional environment.'

CPD has a crucial role in ensuring that you maintain your **technical** and **professional competence** in providing services to clients and service to an employer, and that you keep pace with changes in your work, including changes in the practices, techniques and standards of your profession.

Certain areas of an accountant's **knowledge** are considered **critical** and **must** be kept up-to-date. These areas are:

- Reporting and auditing standards, such as various FRSs, IFRSs and ISAs.

- Ethical codes such as the AAT Code and updates from the IESBA.

- Tax and company legislation such as the annual UK Finance Act and updates to the Companies Act 2006.

- Criminal law that affect accountants. For example the UK Bribery Act 2010, Fraud Act 2006 and Money Laundering Regulations 2007.

- Other regulations affecting accounting, reporting, tax compliance, audit and the regulation of the accounting and finance profession that may be issued by the profession and regulatory organisations.

An accountant is not required to keep themselves up-to-date on all matters that affect the profession. However, they should develop their knowledge of matters that affect their **everyday work**. For example, an accountant in business would not be expected to stay up-to-date on auditing standards.

HOW IT WORKS

Some training needs will emerge in the course of your work. If your organisation introduces new equipment or software, you may need to learn how to use it! You may also identify your own shortcomings (missed deadlines, subjects on which you had to get help from others, times when you did not get the results you wanted) as learning opportunities.

Training needs may also be identified for you, as you get informal performance feedback from your supervisors and colleagues – or through formal appraisal interviews.

Other training needs may be identified as you keep in touch with developments in your professional environment: through the internet, professional journals (such as Accounting Technician), and networking opportunities through your professional body.

There is a huge menu of learning resources and opportunities available for you to use in order to meet you training needs, including:

- Courses, workshops and information seminars.

- Books, quality newspapers, professional journals and technical publications (such as accounting standards, legislation and court reports).

- Videos, CD-ROM and computer software packages for education and training.

- Web sites (for information and accessing training and materials).

- Instruction and procedure manuals used in your organisation (eg to teach you to use equipment and software, or to comply with organisational procedures and practices).

And there are two other very valuable sources of learning:

- **Other people**

  Your superiors and colleagues at work are an excellent potential source of information, advice and instruction/coaching in areas where they are more expert or experienced than you are. They may be able to help you access opportunities (eg nominating you for training programmes or secondments). They are also in an ideal position to offer you feedback (about your strengths and weaknesses, learning/improvement needs and how you are doing in your learning).

  Professional networks provide similar support and guidance within your wider professional sphere.

- **Your own experience**

  'Doing something' is an important development technique! Identify opportunities to try a new technique or approach at work, which you could use as a learning opportunity. If you want to learn to contribute more effectively to meetings, for example, what meetings could you arrange to participate in and observe? Whom could you ask for feedback?

Task 10

If an accountant breaks the rules of their professional body's ethical code they will be liable for a fine under criminal law.

	✓
True	
False	

CHAPTER OVERVIEW

- **Ethical values** are assumptions and beliefs about what constitutes 'right' and 'wrong' behaviour. Individuals, families, national cultures and organisation cultures all develop ethical values and norms.

- **Ethical behaviour** is necessary to comply with law and regulation; to protect the public interest; to protect the reputation and standing of a professional body and its members; and to enable people to live and work together in society.

- **The five fundamental principles** of accountants are:
  - Integrity
  - Objectivity
  - Professional competence and due care
  - Confidentiality and
  - Professional behaviour

- The ethical code sets out a **basic problem solving procedure** for unethical action (the 'conceptual framework'):
  - Identify the threat to the fundamental principles that the action represents
  - Evaluate the threat
  - Apply safeguards to eliminate or reduce the threat
  - If safeguards cannot be applied, decline or discontinue the action

- The **principles-based approach** to ethics encourages case-by-case judgement.

- The accountancy profession is largely self-regulatory, with the professional accountancy bodies each responsible for setting and upholding the ethical standards of their members. This chapter looked at the roles of:
  - FRC
  - IFAC
  - CCAB
  - HMRC
  - NCA

- A **code of conduct** is designed to influence the behaviour of employees; it sets out the procedures to be used in specific ethical situations.

- A **code of practice** is adopted by a profession or organisation to regulate that profession.

- The concept of **business ethics** suggests that businesses and other corporate entities are morally responsible for their actions.

- Finance professionals have a duty to protect the **public interest** and promote **sustainability**. They should consider the **economic (financial)**, **social** and **environmental aspects** to their work.

- As part of their role, finance professionals have a number of **responsibilities** in relation to upholding the principles of **sustainability**.

- There are a number of **operational risks** that businesses face, such as reputation, litigation, process, people, systems, legal and event risk. Many of these risks are affected by unethical behaviour.

- An accountant that is found to have committed **misconduct** is liable for a fine or expulsion from their professional body as well as sanctions from their employer.

- **Continuing professional development** activities ensure that you maintain your technical and professional competence, keeping pace with changes in your work role and the practices, techniques and standards of your profession.

TEST YOUR LEARNING

Respond to the following by selecting the appropriate option.

Test 1

Only individuals can have 'ethical values'.

	✓
True	
False	

Test 2

The accountancy profession needs to maintain standards of conduct and service among its members in order to be able to:

	✓
Enhance the reputation and standing of accountants.	
Limit the number of members that it has.	
Make sure that accountants are able to earn large salaries.	

Test 3

Which of these might (or might be thought to) affect the objectivity of providers of professional accounting services?

	✓
Failure to keep up to date on CPD.	
A personal financial interest in the client's affairs.	
Being negligent or reckless with the accuracy of the information provided to the client.	

Test 4

A client asks you a technical question about accounting standards which you are not sure you are able to answer correctly. 'You are supposed to be an accountant, aren't you?' says the client. 'I need an answer now.' What should you do first?

	✓
Say that you will get back to him when you have looked up the answer.	
Give him the contact details of a friend in your firm who knows all about accounting standards.	
Clarify the limits of your expertise with the client.	

Test 5

Put the four steps of the problem-solving methodology or 'conceptual framework' for ethical conduct into the correct order:

Apply safeguards to eliminate or reduce the threat to an acceptable level.	▼
Evaluate the seriousness of the threat.	▼
Discontinue the action or relationship giving rise to the threat.	▼
Identify a potential threat to a fundamental ethical principle.	▼

Picklist:

1,2,3,4

Test 6

Why are professional standards important?

	✓
It is in the public interest that accountants who fail to comply with standards are prosecuted.	
It is in the public interest that accountancy services are carried out to professional standards.	

Test 7

Which of the following are members of the Consultative Committee of Accountancy Bodies (CCAB)?

	✓
The Institute of Chartered Accountants in England and Wales	
The Institute of Chartered Accountants of Scotland	
Chartered Accountants Ireland	
The Chartered Institute of Management Accountants	
The Association of Chartered Certified Accountants	
The Chartered Institute of Public Finance and Accountancy	
The Association of Accounting Technicians	
The Financial Reporting Council	

Test 8

The UN Brundtland Report regarding sustainability identifies three aspects that accountants have a duty to consider in their work. Which three of the following are they?

	✓
Economic (financial)	
Marketing	
Environmental	
Charity	
Social	
Political	

Test 9

Which type of operational risk can be defined as 'Risk of losses from human error or deliberate actions'.

	✓
Reputational	
Litigation	
Process	
People	
Systems	
Legal	
Event	

Test 10

An accountant is expected to keep themselves up-to-date in all aspects of accountancy, even in areas outside their area of work.

	✓
True	
False	

chapter 2:
BEHAVING IN AN ETHICAL MANNER I

chapter coverage 📖

Accountants may work for a commercial organisation in business or in practice with an accountancy firm. This means they perform a range of roles from processing invoices to preparing and reporting financial and other information, which their employer and third parties may rely on. They may also be responsible for financial management and advice on a range of business-related matters.

Where possible we shall consider ethical guidance applicable to each type of accountant together. Remember, you should be aware of all the rules, not just the ones applicable to your current role.

In this and the next chapter we shall build on the ethical principles which were introduced in Chapter 1 and identify how they should be applied in practice.

The topics covered are:

✍ Acting ethically

✍ Safeguards to protect against threats to fundamental principles

✍ The accountant/client relationship

ACTING ETHICALLY

You should have realised from Chapter 1 that accounting matters often require the use of personal and professional judgement, and opinions as to the best or 'right' way to handle them can sincerely differ. Moreover, people need to develop their own ethical and technical judgement, as part of their own personal and continuing professional development. We shall now look at what behaving ethically means in practice beginning with acting with integrity, honesty, fairness and sensitivity in your dealings with clients, suppliers, colleagues and others.

Integrity

Accountants have a key role in preparing **financial statements**. Those who work in business may also prepare and report on a range of **information** for use by management and others – for example forecasts and budgets, costings, pricing calculations and management/business reports.

There is a clear need to apply the fundamental principles of integrity (not presenting untruthful or misleading information), confidentiality (not disclosing confidential information), professional competence and due care (preparing and presenting information in accordance with financial reporting and other applicable professional standards), professional behaviour (avoiding action that brings the profession into disrepute), and objectivity (presenting information free from bias or self-interest).

The AAT Code provides us with advice on how financial information should be presented. It states that the accountant should prepare and present the information '**fairly, honestly and in accordance with relevant professional standards** so that the information will be understood in its context'.

Honesty

Honesty simply means being truthful and not acting in a manner intended to mislead or deceive others. Using the work phone for personal calls when not permitted to do so and taking 'sick days' when you are not sick are fairly common behaviours – and your organisation's culture may have come to regard them as 'harmless' or even 'normal'. But they are still dishonest. Just because 'everyone does it' does not make it right.

Task 1

List some examples of behaviours that would be considered dishonest for you either as a student accountant or as an employee in a work context. Include an example of dishonest behaviour that the perpetrator might not even be aware was dishonest.

Fairness

Acting fairly means treating others equally. The increasing diversity of the modern workplace requires fairness, mutual respect and open communication, as the basis for constructive working relationships. As an accountant you not only have an ethical reason to be fair, but there is legislation in the UK which prohibits discrimination and harassment on a variety of grounds. These include race and colour, sex and sexual orientation, and religious belief.

Sensitivity

Sensitivity essentially means respecting another's right to confidentiality and privacy. Employers have specific duties to respect the confidentiality of employee information, but this should be extended to individual relationships – particularly if you have authority over others (and may be involved in counselling, disciplinary or grievance interviews).

SAFEGUARDS TO PROTECT AGAINST THREATS TO FUNDAMENTAL PRINCIPLES

We saw in Chapter 1 that professional accountancy ethical codes identify five threats to compliance with the fundamental principles and some safeguards designed to protect against such threats. To recap, the threats identified are:

- Self-interest
- Self-review
- Familiarity
- Intimidation
- Advocacy

Since members who work in an accountancy practice are affected by different threats to those working in a commercial business, most codes make specific recommendations to each situation.

The first two of the following tables summarise the main threats to members in practice and business. The third table identifies possible safeguards that can be applied in the work environment by both members in practice and members in business.

Threats: members in practice

Members in practice	
Threat category	**Specific threats**
Self-interest	■ Having a financial interest or joint financial interest in a client
	■ Depending upon a client's fees for a significant portion of your income
	■ Having a close personal relationship with a client
	■ Having concerns about losing a client
	■ Potential employment with a client
	■ Contingent fees (these are fees that depend on the results of the work)
	■ Receiving a loan from a client or from its directors or officers
	■ Discovery of a significant error when re-evaluating the work of a member of staff
Self-review	■ Discovery of a significant error when re-evaluating your work
	■ Reporting on the operation of systems after being involved in designing them
	■ Preparing the data which is used to generate reports which you are required to check
	■ Being, or having recently been, a director or officer of a client you are now auditing or being employed by the client in a position to exert significant influence over the subject matter of the engagement
	■ Performing a service for the client that directly affects the subject matter of the engagement

Members in practice	
Threat category	**Specific threats**
Familiarity	▪ Having a close or personal relationship with a director or officer of a client or with an employee of the client who is in a position to exert significant influence over the engagement
	▪ A former partner of a firm now employed in a senior position of the client so they are able to exert significant influence on the direction of the work
	▪ Accepting significant gifts or preferential treatment from a client
	▪ Long association of senior personnel with the client
Intimidation	▪ Threat of dismissal, replacement, or litigation in respect of an engagement
	▪ Pressure to reduce the quality of your work in order to keep fees down
	▪ Pressure to agree with the judgement of an employee of the client who has more expertise on a specific matter
	▪ Threat by an assurance client of not awarding planned non-assurance contract to the firm if it disagrees with accounting treatment for a particular transaction
Advocacy	▪ Acting on behalf of a client which is in dispute with a third party

Threats: members in business

Members in business	
Threat category	**Specific threats**
Self-interest	■ Having a financial interest (eg shares or a loan) in the employer
	■ Financial incentives and rewards based on results or profits (including commissions)
	■ Opportunity to use corporate assets to your own advantage
	■ Threats to your job security or promotion prospects
	■ Commercial pressure from outside the organisation
Self-review	■ Being asked to review data or justify/evaluate business decisions that you have been involved in preparing/making
Familiarity	■ Having a close or personal relationship with someone who may benefit from your influence
	■ Long association with a business contact, which may influence your decisions
	■ Acceptance of a significant gift or preferential treatment, which might be thought to influence your decisions
Intimidation	■ Threat of dismissal or replacement over a disagreement over the application of an accounting principle or the manner in which financial information is reported
	■ A dominant individual attempting to influence your decisions
Advocacy	■ There is unlikely to be a significant advocacy threat to employees of an organisation. This is because they are entitled and expected to promote the employer's position or viewpoint, as part of furthering its legitimate goals and objectives, though as professional accountants they also have a duty to society (the public interest) as a whole

Safeguards

The following table summarises some key safeguards in the work environment available to both members in practice and members in business.

Members in practice	Members in business
■ Development of a leadership culture in the firm that stresses the importance of compliance with the fundamental principles and acting in the public interest	■ The employer's structures, systems and processes
■ Policies and procedures to implement and monitor quality control and require compliance with the fundamental principles	■ The employer's own ethical codes and codes of conduct ■ Disciplinary processes ■ Strong internal controls
■ Policies that identify threats to the fundamental principles, evaluate their significance and identify safeguards to reduce or eliminate them	■ Quality/performance monitoring systems ■ Recruitment, selection, appraisal, promotion, training and reward systems that all highlight ethics and competence as key criteria
■ Documented independence policies for firms that perform assurance engagements	■ Leaders that communicate and model ethical behaviour and expectations
■ Policies and procedures to identify interests and relationships between the firm or employees and clients	■ Policies and procedures supporting employees in raising ethical concerns without fear of retribution ('whistle blowing')
■ Policies to monitor fee dependence	■ Forums for discussing ethical issues at work (eg an ethics committee)
■ Using different partners and teams to provide assurance and non-assurance services	■ The opportunity to consult with another professional (in confidence) if required
■ Procedures that prevent non-team members influencing an engagement	
■ Timely communication of all policies and procedures and providing education and training in all policies and procedures	
■ Specified senior management in charge of quality control system	

Members in practice	Members in business
■ Disciplinary procedures for failing to comply with policies and procedures	
■ Published policies and procedures on whistle blowing	
■ Engagement-specific safeguards (eg internal review, consulting a third party, discussing ethical issues with those charged with governance at the client, involving another firm to perform/re-perform part of the engagement, rotating senior assurance team members)	
■ Reliance on the client's safeguards (sole reliance on these is not possible)	

Task 2

An accountant who has been told that they will be subject to disciplinary action unless they interpret an accounting standard in a particular way, faces which of the following threats to their ethical principles?

	✓
Self-review	
Intimidation	
Familiarity	
Advocacy	

THE ACCOUNTANT/CLIENT RELATIONSHIP

Acting with integrity, honesty and fairness does not just apply to the performance of your work as an accountant. There are a number of matters that relate to relationships with clients that are relevant to members in practice.

Professional appointment and transfer of clients

For all sorts of reasons, a client may wish to **change** from one professional adviser to another. They may be relocating, or looking for more (or different) specialised expertise – or lower fees. Where a client is looking to switch advisers, the key ethical issue is how to **protect the interests of all parties**, by ensuring that information relevant to the change of appointment is properly exchanged.

An important point to bear in mind when accepting a new appointment is to ensure that doing so does not breach any of the **fundamental principles**. Therefore, **before accepting a new client**, accountants must consider whether there would be any threats arising from accepting that client.

When taking on a **new client**, the accountant should consider whether they will have the resources (competent staff, time, technical expertise) to give the client a quality service? Are there potential **threats to objectivity** (eg are they related to an officer of the client company) or **confidentiality** (eg the client is a competitor of another client, and might pressure you to disclose information)?

A number of threats can occur when an accountant loses a client to another practice. For example, **confidentiality** may be an issue if both accountants are well known to each other, **familiarity** may be a problem if the accountant/client relationship has developed over a long period of time and there may be a **self-interest** threat if the client provides a large proportion of the practice's income and this would be lost if they leave.

Money laundering prevention procedures

When acquiring clients, and also when working with continuing clients, the accountant must always be aware of the risk that their services are being used to facilitate **money laundering or terrorist financing**. The applicable anti-money laundering legislation in the UK consists of:

- **The Proceeds of Crime Act 2002** (as amended)
- **The Terrorism Act 2000** (as amended)
- **The Money Laundering Regulations 2007** (as amended)

The AAT has also provided its own guidance on compliance with **obligations** under the Money Laundering Regulations 2007. These obligations include customer due diligence on clients, reporting money laundering or terrorist financing, and record keeping. Failure to comply with these requirements results in a breach of professional behaviour.

We will look at **customer due diligence** now (since this must take place when accountants take on new clients), but we will look at money laundering in detail later in this Text, together with other aspects of compliance with money laundering legislation. Therefore it may be useful to return to this section again once you have covered the material in later chapters.

Customer due diligence provisions of the **Money Laundering Regulations 2007** will apply in certain circumstances and when the relevant monetary threshold for a related occasional transaction (or series of transactions) is exceeded.

The regulations state that customer due diligence **must** be applied when:

- A member enters a professional relationship with a client which will have an element of duration

- The member acts in relation to a transaction or series of related transactions amounting to, or more than, €15,000 (or the equivalent in sterling)

- There is a suspicion of money laundering or terrorist financing

- Where there are doubts about previously obtained customer identification; or

- At appropriate times to existing clients on a risk sensitive basis.

Customer due diligence must be carried out on all **new** clients **before** providing any services to them. The **one exception** to this rule is where undertaking customer due diligence would interrupt the normal conduct of business and the risk of money laundering and terrorist financing is very low. In this case, members must find out who the client claims to be before starting work and complete customer due diligence procedures as soon as reasonably possible afterwards.

For **new clients**, customer due diligence will start with finding out who the client claims to be and obtaining evidence to verify this.

Members also need to **obtain evidence about** individuals who exceed the ownership threshold and so are classified as **beneficial owners** of the new client. Beneficial owners are those **who own 25% or more of the client or the transaction property.**

Information must also be obtained about the **purpose and intended nature of the transaction.** Evidence obtained may be documentary, data or information from a reliable independent source (or a combination of all of these forms of evidence).

A key point to note is that if customer due diligence cannot be completed (unless the exception described earlier is relevant), the accountant must not act for the client and must consider whether they need to make an internal report to their firm's Money Laundering Reporting Officer (MLRO) or an external report (Suspicious Activity Report, SAR) to the National Crime Agency (NCA), if they are a sole practitioner (these reports are covered in Chapter 4).

For **existing clients**, on-going monitoring must be undertaken. This involves carrying out appropriate customer due diligence procedures on any transactions that appear inconsistent with existing knowledge of the client, and keeping customer due diligence records up to date.

As stated earlier, customer due diligence must also be applied where there doubts arise over the validity of previously obtained customer identification information.

Recommendations and referrals

A satisfied client may introduce others to your practice, and that's fine. You might also offer a **commission**, fee or reward to your employees for bringing in a new client. But you should never offer financial incentives to a third party to introduce clients (a referral fee or commission) – unless:

- The client is aware that the third party has been paid for the referral; and

- The third party is also bound by professional (or comparable) ethical standards, and can be trusted to carry out the introduction with integrity.

Accountants might also pay a **referral fee** to obtain a client. This could arise in the situation where the client continues as a client of another firm but requires specialist services not offered by that firm. Accepting such commissions and referral fees can give rise to **self-interest threats** to objectivity and professional competence and due care.

Task 3

According to professional ethics, before accepting a new client relationship, an accountant in practice must consider:

	✓
How profitable the relationship will be.	
Whether acceptance would create any threats to compliance with the fundamental principles.	
Whether the client's directors meet the firm's moral and ethical standards.	

Constraints on the services you can supply

Another point worth noting is that, for various reasons, you may not want to take on every client that approaches or is introduced to you! For example they may not offer sufficient profit or the work may be too specialised for your firm.

The **main constraint** on the services that an accountant can supply is that they should not take on work that they are not **competent to perform**. This is to protect against them breaching the principle of professional competence and due care.

It is important to note that there are certain **services that an accountant cannot legally offer** unless they are **authorised** to do so by the **relevant regulatory body** in the UK. These services, known as **'reserved areas'** are:

- **External audit** of UK limited companies, or where the services of a registered auditor are required;

- **Investment business** (including agency for a building society) and the provision of corporate financial advice; and

- **Insolvency practice** (company liquidations and administration).

In addition, while you are providing public accountancy services, you should not at the same time engage in any other business, occupation or activity that:

- May threaten your **integrity**, **objectivity** or **independence**, or the reputation of the profession.

- May prevent you from conducting your practice according to the technical and **ethical standards** of the profession.

When considering accepting a particular engagement, you must also bear in mind any threat to the principle of **professional competence and due care**. You should only agree to provide services that you are competent to perform – or for which you can obtain the help, training or supervision you require in order to be able to perform competently.

Safeguards may include:

- Making sure that you have an adequate understanding of the client's business, and the specific requirements of the engagement.

- Making sure that you have, or can obtain, relevant knowledge and experience, help or advice.

- Consulting an expert, if required.

- Making sure the timescales for the task are realistic (so you are not under undue time pressure).

- Assigning staff with the necessary skills.

- Complying with appropriate quality control policies and procedures.

Conflicts of interest

As we saw earlier, conflicts of interest can result from a number of circumstances and preventing conflicts are key to ensuring **professional distance** is maintained between the accountant and client.

According to 100.17 of the AAT Code, 'a professional accountant may be faced with a **conflict of interest** when undertaking a professional activity. A conflict of interest creates a threat to objectivity and may create threats to the other fundamental principles.

Such threats may be created when:

The professional accountant undertakes a professional activity related to a particular matter for two or more parties whose interests with respect to that matter are in conflict; or

The interests of the professional accountant with respect to a particular matter and the interests of a party for whom the professional accountant undertakes a professional activity related to that matter are in conflict.[1]

The code (Sections 220.2 and 310.2) provides the following **examples of threats to conflicts of interest**.

Members in practice	Members in business
■ Providing a transaction advisory service to a client seeking to acquire an audit client of the firm, where the firm has obtained confidential information during the course of the audit that may be relevant to the transaction.	■ Serving in a management or governance position for two employing organisations and acquiring confidential information from one employing organisation that could be used by the professional accountant to the advantage or disadvantage of the other employing organisation.
■ Advising two clients at the same time who are competing to acquire the same company where the advice might be relevant to the parties' competitive positions.	■ Undertaking a professional activity for each of two parties in a partnership employing the professional accountant to assist them to dissolve their partnership.
■ Providing services to both a vendor and a purchaser in relation to the same transaction.	■ Preparing financial information for certain members of management of the entity employing the professional accountant who are seeking to undertake a management buy-out.
■ Preparing valuations of assets for two parties who are in an adversarial position with respect to the assets.	
■ Representing two clients regarding the same matter who are in a legal dispute with each other, such as during divorce proceedings or the dissolution of a partnership.	■ Being responsible for selecting a vendor for the accountant's employing organisation when an immediate family member of the professional accountant could benefit financially from the transaction.
■ Providing an assurance report for a licensor on royalties due under a license agreement when at the same time advising the licensee of the correctness of the amounts payable.	■ Serving in a governance capacity in an employing organisation that is approving certain investments for the company where one of those specific investments will increase the value of the personal investment portfolio of

Members in practice	Members in business
■ Advising a client to invest in a business in which, for example, the spouse of the professional accountant in public practice has a financial interest.	the professional accountant or an immediate family member.
■ Providing strategic advice to a client on its competitive position while having a joint venture or similar interest with a major competitor of the client.	
■ Advising a client on the acquisition of a business which the firm is also interested in acquiring.	
■ Advising a client on the purchase of a product or service while having a royalty or commission agreement with one of the potential vendors of that product or service.	

When identifying whether a conflict of interest exists or may be created, a professional accountant should take reasonable steps to determine the **nature of the relevant interests**, the **relationships between the parties involved** and **the nature of the activity** and **its implication for relevant parties**.

The activities, interests and relationships may **change over time**. The professional accountant should remain alert to such changes for the purposes of identifying circumstances that might create a conflict of interest.

If a **conflict of interest is identified**, the professional accountant shall evaluate the **significance of relevant interests** or **relationships** and the **significance of the threats** created by undertaking the professional activity or activities.

In general, the more direct the connection between the professional activity and the matter on which the parties' interests are in conflict, the more significant the threat to objectivity and compliance with the other fundamental principles will be.

If any threats are identified which are **not clearly insignificant**, then the following safeguards could be applied to members in business and practice as appropriate:

- Using separate engagement teams.

- Creating different areas of practice within the firm that prevent the passing of confidential information.

- Having procedures in place to prevent access to information.

- Regular reviews of the application of safeguards by a senior person not involved with those engagements.

- Have key judgements and conclusions reviewed by a professional accountant not connected with the service.

- Restructuring responsibilities and duties.

- Have work supervised by a non-executive director.

- Withdraw from decision-making where a conflict exists.

- Consult third parties such as professional bodies, accountants and legal counsel

The above safeguards essentially means that when you accept a new appointment, or become aware of changes in the circumstances of an existing client, you should check whether this might create a conflict of interest with another client. **The general principle is that the interests of one client must not have a negative effect on the interests of another.**

If safeguards cannot reduce the threat to an **acceptable level**, the professional accountant shall decline to undertake or discontinue the professional activity that would result in the conflict of interest; or shall terminate the relevant relationships or dispose of relevant interests to eliminate the threat or reduce it to an acceptable level.

Dealing with a conflict of interest

An example of a conflict of interest would be where an accountant has two client companies that are in **direct competition**. In the course of their work, the accountant may have to produce disclosures or reports about one client that might benefit the other.

Such conflicts create an ethical dilemma for the accountant, because it is impossible in such a case to act in the best interests of both clients at the same time – if they are required to make disclosures about one client, how is another, a competitor, to be expected to avoid making good use of them? It may also be an issue for a client if they think there may be a risk that another client may (through the accountant) get hold of sensitive information.

If there is likely to be such a conflict of interest, the accountant should:

- Put safeguards in place to avoid the negative effects, if possible.

- Avoid new appointments that might negatively affect existing clients.

- Disclose enough information to both parties, so that they can make a decision over whether to enter into (or continue) an engagement with them.

In large firms, this may be less of a problem, as completely separate teams can work on different client accounts. This is sometimes called 'building a **Chinese wall**' within the firm, between client affairs.

Task 4

The situation where a firm of accountants has two clients which compete with each other is likely to create a conflict of interest for the accountant.

	✔
True	
False	

Second opinions

In some instances, a client of another firm may seek your opinion on the advice they have received from that firm. This is known as a **second opinion**. There are a variety of ethical issues that this situation raises, such as your competence to do the work. When dealing with a request for a second opinion, the accountant should evaluate the significance of any threats and apply appropriate safeguards if the threats are significant.

Appropriate safeguards could include:

- Seeking the client's permission to contact the existing accountant.

- Describing the limitations surrounding any opinion in communications with the client.

- Providing the existing accountant with a copy of the opinion.

If the client does not give permission for the firm to contact the existing accountant, you need to consider whether it would still be appropriate to provide the opinion requested.

Fees and other types of remuneration

Accountants provide services for clients in return for fees which they usually charge on a **time basis**. This means the actual charges a client must pay are dependent on how much time the accountant takes to perform their work and how much they charge per hour. The ethical issues concerning fees are usually related to setting the hourly charge for different levels of staff and accurate time keeping.

Accountants can quote whatever fee they want to, but there are threats to the fundamental principles when fees quoted are so low that it is not possible to carry out the engagement with **professional competence and due care**. Safeguards include informing the client of the terms of the engagement including the basis on which fees are charged, and assigning appropriate time and qualified staff to the engagement.

As mentioned above, professional fees will normally be calculated on the basis of an agreed appropriate **rate per hour** or **per day** for the time of each person involved on the assignment. The 'appropriate rate' should take into account the skill, knowledge, experience, time and responsibility involved in the work. It also assumes that individuals give a 'fair hour's work for a fair hour's fees', in other words, that the work is efficiently planned and managed, so that clients get value for money. It may not be possible to state accurately in advance what the total charge for work will be. If there is any likelihood that the fee will end up being substantially higher than you estimate, do not give the client that estimate – or at least make it clear that the actual amount may be substantially higher.

It may, however, be necessary to charge a **pre-arranged fee** for the assignment, based on your estimate of how long the work will take; this is quite acceptable, as long as the fee is fair for the work – and the work is fulfilled on that basis.

Contingent fees

Contingent fees (or percentage fees) are those calculated on a predetermined basis relating to the outcome or result of a transaction or the result of the work performed.

This is customary for some types of engagement where **professional help** is required to gain the client funds (eg selling an asset or recovering debts). If the assignment is not successful, the client may not be able to pay – and therefore, a percentage fee, contingent on results, is the only way they could gain access to professional services.

Be aware, however, that you **cannot offer financial reporting services on a contingent fee basis** – depending on a specific finding or result being obtained would present a major threat to your professional objectivity.

Again, safeguards need to be applied for any identified significant threats. These include:

- Advance written agreement on fees.

- Disclosure to intended users of the work performed and basis of remuneration.

- Quality control policies and procedures.

- Review by an independent third party of the work done.

Expenses

Out-of-pocket expenses that are directly related to the work performed for a particular client (such as travelling expenses) may be charged to the client, for reimbursement, in addition to professional fees.

HOW IT WORKS

You have just had a phone call from a prospective new client, asking about fees. You offer a free-of-charge consultation to discuss the matter. The client has recently left his job to become a freelance photographer; in the first instance, he requires an accountant to prepare financial statements and tax returns, and to advise on financial management.

'How much will you charge per year?' he asks. You explain that your fees are based on an hourly rate, which you quote to him.

'Yes, but how much in total?' he asks. You explain that it will depend on the work involved. You could make an estimate – but you would need authorisation from the partner to whom you report. Moreover, the client would have to be aware that the amount actually billed could be substantially higher, for example, if the client's business arrangements proved to be different from that anticipated.

'Do you reduce the fee if you don't save me as much tax as you thought?' the client asks. You explain that you cannot set a contingent fee on this basis, nor can you make any promises in relation to tax savings. 'What about if I get you to help me with a proposal for an Arts Grant that's available for photographers?' he persists. 'Will you accept a commission on that, instead of an hourly rate?' You agree that this would be possible.

'What about expenses?' pursues the client. 'Will I be paying for all this nice office space?' 'No', you explain. 'This is covered in our overall charge-out rates; you will only be charged out-of-pocket expenses directly related to my work for you.'

Marketing professional services

To attract new clients, accountancy practices may **advertise** their services to the public and businesses. As in any form of advertising there are risks of misrepresenting your services and of making claims that damage the competition, either deliberately or negligently. In other words how a practice advertises itself, and how it tries to win an advantage over its competitors, is an ethical issue.

Accountants must not bring the profession into **disrepute** when marketing their services. This includes being **honest and truthful** and not making **exaggerated claims** for the services offered, qualifications or experience, and not making **disparaging references or unsubstantiated comparisons** to the work of others.

The general principle is that a **professional practice**, and its individual accountants, need to:

- Project an image consistent with the 'dignity' (the high ethical and technical standards) of the profession.

- Maintain integrity in all promotional actions and statements.

Aggressive following up of contacts and leads is considered good marketing in some contexts – but it can be both counter-productive (by putting clients off) and unethical if you are promoting professional services. If you contact or approach potential clients directly and repeatedly, or otherwise in a 'pushy' manner, you may be open to a complaint of **harassment**.

Task 5

Advertising low fees to attract new clients is permitted under the ethical code providing they are justified by pointing out that competing firms are over-charging for their services.

	✓
True	
False	

CHAPTER OVERVIEW

- **Behaving ethically** means acting with integrity, honesty, fairness and sensitivity in dealings with clients, suppliers, colleagues and others.

- Accountants face numerous **threats** against the five fundamental ethical principles. These threats can be classified as self-interest, self-review, familiarity, intimidation and advocacy.

- There are a number of **safeguards** against the threats accountants face. Some are described in the ethical code, other sources of safeguards include the law and policies and procedures set out by their employer.

- There are a number of important principles and procedures to follow when an accountant in practice **acquires new clients**. At all times the law must be followed and respect and dignity should be shown to competitors and the accounting profession. In particular, rules cover:

  - Constraints on the services that can be provided
  - Dealing with conflicts of interest
  - Transferring clients
  - Money laundering regulations
  - Fees and receiving commission for recommending new clients
  - Giving second opinions
  - Marketing professional services

TEST YOUR LEARNING

Respond to the following by selecting the appropriate option.

Test 1

The discovery of a significant error whilst re-evaluating your work will give rise to a self-interest threat.

	✔
True	
False	

Test 2

Accepting payment for introducing a client to another firm can give rise to which of the following threats to the fundamental ethical principles?

	✔
Self-interest	
Self-review	
Advocacy	
Familiarity	
Intimidation	

Test 3

Which of these represents a threat to professional competence and due care?

	✔
Providing a second opinion.	
Accepting a gift from a supplier.	

Test 4

| ▼ | forms part of UK anti-money laundering legislation.

Picklist:

The Bribery Act
The Terrorism Act
The Theft Act

chapter 3:
BEHAVING IN AN ETHICAL MANNER II

chapter coverage 📖

In this chapter, we continue our look at some of the specific situations that may be encountered in public practice or when providing accounting services.

The topics covered are:

- Objectivity and professional independence
- Acting with sufficient expertise
- Policies for handling client monies
- Confidentiality and disclosure

OBJECTIVITY AND PROFESSIONAL INDEPENDENCE

An accountant has a duty to maintain an appropriate **professional distance** between their work and their personal life at all times. This is required in order to be able to act objectively, ie independence and objectivity are linked. We have already seen the need for independence when we looked specifically at conflicts of interest in Chapter 2 but the ethical code provides wider rules that you must follow in this regard.

Objectivity and independence – members in practice

The fundamental principle of objectivity requires accountants not to compromise their **professional judgement** due to bias, conflict of interest or undue influence of others.

The ethical code provides advice on how accountants can **maintain their objectivity** in relation to all services. It states that they must consider whether there are any threats to objectivity specifically from having **interests in, or relationships with, a client or directors, officers or employees of a client**. For example, a familiarity threat to objectivity may be created from a close personal or business relationship.

Where significant threats to objectivity are identified, safeguards have to be applied to eliminate or reduce the threats to an acceptable level. These could include the following:

- Withdrawing from the engagement team
- Supervisory procedures
- Terminating the financial/business relationship
- Discussions with senior management in the firm
- Discussions with those charged with governance at the client

If there are no safeguards that can eliminate or reduce the threat to an acceptable level, the engagement must be declined or terminated. Before you decide to accept a new appointment or engagement (or to continue with an existing one), you need to consider:

- Potential **threats to objectivity** that may arise – or appear to arise – from the context and/or the people connected with the work.

- What **safeguards** can be used to offset the threats – and whether these are sufficient to protect your objectivity and independence.

There are specific situations or threats associated with a lack of professional distance between professional duties and personal life ie a lack of independence. These can be relevant to members in business and in practice. We have already considered one such threat – a conflict of interest. Now we look at others.

Financial interests (relevant to members in business)

There are a number of ways in which an accountant in business could gain financially from their activities for an employer – and many of these might pose a **self-interest threat** to fundamental ethical principles such as integrity, confidentiality, or (especially) objectivity. Other potential threats might be where the accountant, or someone close to the accountant, holds a financial interest (eg a loan or shares), is eligible for a profit-related bonus or holds, or is eligible for, share options in the employing organisation. The decisions and reports made or influenced by an accountant may affect the value of such interests (eg by inflating profit figures or enhancing share values).

A **financial interest** can be defined as 'an interest in an equity or other security, debenture, loan or other debt instrument of an entity, including rights and obligations to acquire such an interest and derivatives directly related to such interest'. Financial interests can be direct or indirect.

A **direct financial interest** is 'a financial interest:

- Owned directly by and under the control of an individual or entity or

- Beneficially owned through a collective investment vehicle, estate, trust or

- Other intermediary over which the individual or entity has control.'

An **indirect financial interest** is 'a financial interest beneficially owned through a collective investment vehicle, estate, trust or other intermediary over which the individual or entity has no control'.

Accountants in business should **evaluate the nature** of the financial interest, ie evaluating the significance of the financial interest and whether it is direct or indirect.

If significant threats are present (ie the interest is direct and of high value), safeguards will have to be put in place. If you think there may be an issue, you should consult with your supervisor, and perhaps with higher authorities. This might include, for example, an independent committee to set remuneration (for senior managers) and the need to disclose relevant interests and share trading to the officials in charge of corporate governance in your organisation.

Other safeguards might include consulting those charged with governance or relevant professional bodies, internal and external audit procedures, and up-to-date training on ethical issues and the legislation relevant to potential insider dealing.

The bottom line is not to **manipulate** information, and not to **use** confidential information, for your own financial gain.

Gifts, hospitality and inducements

One of the key **threats to independence** and **objectivity** (and the appearance of independence and objectivity) is accepting gifts, services, favours or hospitality from parties who may have an interest in the outcome of your work:

- A work colleague (if working in business)

- A client (if working in practice)

- Any party with a current or proposed contractual relationship with your employing organisation: contractors and suppliers for example

These may be (or may be seen as) an attempt to **influence the objectivity** of your decisions, or to make you do or not do something. Whilst you might not actually be influenced by them, there is a wider issue of **public perception.** It is important for the profession that accountants are seen to be above suspicion of being influenced. It is also an issue for business organisations and accountancy practices, and they often include rules on dealing with gifts and hospitality in their own codes of conduct.

You do not personally have to be the intended recipient; gifts to your spouse or dependent children are assumed to be equally compromising.

Note also that if you offer gifts, favours or hospitality, this may be seen as an attempt to unethically influence others. Does this mean that you cannot accept a bottle of wine at Christmas, or a calendar from a supplier? No. The gift needs to be significant enough that it could be reasonably perceived, by a third party who has all the facts, as likely to influence your judgement.

Guidance for members in business

Accepting **significant inducements** can give rise to self-interest and intimidation threats to objectivity and confidentiality. The question of whether an inducement is significant is one of professional judgement and to this end, the AAT Code gives the following advice:

350.3 'The existence and significance of such threats will depend on the nature, value and intent behind the offer. If a reasonable and informed third party, having knowledge of all relevant information, would consider the inducement insignificant and not intended to encourage unethical behaviour, then a member in business may conclude that the offer is made in the normal course of business and may generally conclude that there is no significant threat to compliance with the fundamental principles.'

Possible **safeguards** to eliminate or reduce any significant threats to an acceptable level could include the following:

- Informing senior management of the firm or those charged with governance at the client.

- Informing third parties such as a professional body.

- Advising close or personal relations or associates of possible threats and safeguards.

Sometimes, members in business are expected to offer inducements to influence the judgement of others or a decision-making process or to get confidential information. The AAT Code explicitly states that accountants in business must not offer inducements to **improperly influence** the professional judgement of a third party.

Guidance for members in practice

Accepting gifts and hospitality can give rise to **self-interest** and **intimidation** threats to objectivity. Again, the question of whether the gift or hospitality is significant depends on professional judgement and the Code provides the same advice on this as for accountants in business.

Some appropriate safeguards to eliminate or reduce the threat to an acceptable level could include:

- Informing your boss if an offer (other than something clearly insignificant or customary) has been made.

- Informing your boss if a close friend or personal relation of yours is employed by a competitor or potential supplier of your organisation (because an inappropriate appeal to your relationship, friendship or loyalty may be a form of 'inducement').

The Bribery Act 2010

How to deal with gifts, hospitality and inducements has long been an issue in both the UK and abroad. The problem is where to draw the line between legally developing and maintaining mutually beneficial business relations and the criminal acts of bribery and corruption.

The **Bribery Act 2010** is UK legislation that came into force in 2011 and applies to both individuals and organisations. The legislation has been dubbed 'the toughest anti-corruption legislation in the world' and seeks to provide a framework to make the distinction clear.

The Bribery Act 2010 introduces **four offences** to UK law:

- Bribing another person
- Being bribed
- Bribing a foreign public official
- Failure by a commercial organisation to prevent bribery

Bribery occurs when a person offers, promises or gives a financial or other advantage to another individual in exchange for improperly performing a relevant function or activity.

The offence of **being bribed** is defined as requesting, accepting or agreeing to receive such an advantage, in exchange for improperly performing such a function or activity.

The Bribery Act 2010 does not explain what **'financial or other advantage'** means but it could include contracts, non-monetary gifts or offers of employment. **'Relevant function or activity'** is explained in the legislation as covering 'any function of a public nature; any activity connected with a business, trade or profession; any activity performed in the course of a person's employment; or any activity performed on or behalf of a body of persons whether corporate or unincorporated'. The Act explains that the activity is improperly performed when the expectation of good faith or impartiality has been breached, or when it has been performed in a way not expected of a person in a position of trust.

Organisations need to demonstrate that there are **controls in place** to mitigate the risk of bribery, should the business or an employee be accused of bribery.

The **penalties** imposed if individuals or companies are found guilty of bribery are severe. Individuals may be imprisoned for up to ten years and face an unlimited fine. Companies may face an unlimited fine. In addition to this, there will be the associated bad publicity and loss of reputation.

Task 1

You have been recently employed as a payables ledger clerk for a construction company. Your manager has been granted ten tickets to attend the Ashes Test Match at Lords Cricket Ground, London, in a corporate hospitality box by a consultancy firm that is bidding for the contract to design your company's new computer system.

Describe the factors which will determine whether there is an ethical issue arising from the granting of the tickets.

Based on those factors, state whether you think the situation results in an ethical issue for:

- You
- Your manager
- Both you and your manager
- Neither you or your manager

HOW IT WORKS

At a training workshop, you are asking other accounts staff to discuss their ethical questions and concerns.

- One accounting technician feels it is dishonest to use work time and systems for personal emails. Another argues that this is part of the 'psychological contract': staff get paid slightly under market rate, so it's understood that small 'perks' can be taken advantage of, as long as the system is not abused. Lively discussion ensues as to where the line is between 'use' and 'abuse'.

- The first speaker accuses the other of dishonesty. You intervene and emphasise that no blame can be attached, since this has been a 'grey area' in the firm. Later, you take the accuser aside privately, and suggest that he gives some thought to the ethics of publicly criticising a professional colleague.

- One receivables ledger clerk compares your company's ethics favourably to those of his previous employer, and begins to detail its attempts to infringe copyright. You intervene, and remind him that he owes a duty of confidentiality to his former employer.

- There is some discussion about workplace humour. A cost accountant has been hurt by constant jokes about his religion.

  The others tell him to 'lighten up' but you draw the group's attention to the laws on religious harassment. The group grows thoughtful...

BPP
LEARNING MEDIA

- Later, one of the staff approaches you and says that he has an ethical dilemma. He exaggerated his past work experience on his CV when applying for the job, and was not questioned on it in the interview. Now, however, he is being given tasks which he is not sure he is competent to perform correctly – but is afraid that if he says anything, he will be accused of getting the job under false pretences, and fired. You advise him to speak honestly with his supervisor – or at least to own up to being 'rusty' in this area: the important thing is not to take on tasks beyond his ability, and to get the help he needs.

We now look at this last issue, of acting with sufficient expertise, in more detail.

ACTING WITH SUFFICIENT EXPERTISE

We now look at the issue of acting with sufficient expertise.

Accountants in business

The AAT Code states the following in relation to **accountants in business:**

> 330.1 'The fundamental principle of professional competence and due care requires that a member in business shall only undertake significant tasks for which the member in business has, or can obtain, sufficient specific training or experience. However, if the member in business has adequate support, usually in the form of supervision from an individual who has the necessary training and experience, then it may be possible to undertake appropriate significant tasks. A member in business shall not intentionally mislead an employer as to the level of expertise or experience possessed and a member in business shall seek appropriate expert advice and assistance when required.'

A member in business may be asked to undertake a wide range of tasks in the course of their work. Some of these tasks may be significant in their potential impact on the organisation and its stakeholders. Some of them may be tasks for which they have had little or no specific training or direct experience; tasks relating to a specialist field of accountancy, say, or to a specific industry sector or organisation type (such as charities) – or even unfamiliar software and systems.

Potential **threats** to the principle of competence and due care include: time pressure (when there may not be enough time to complete a task properly); insufficient or inaccurate information; lack of resources (eg equipment or help); or your own lack of experience, knowledge or training.

These threats may not be significant if you are working as part of a team, or under supervision, or on a comparatively low-level task. If they *are* significant, however, you may need to apply safeguards to eliminate them or reduce them to an acceptable level. These could include some of the following:

- Obtaining additional advice or training.

- Ensuring you have enough time to do your work.

- Getting help from someone with the relevant knowledge.

- Consulting with superiors, independent experts or the relevant professional body.

Much as you may enjoy a 'challenge', take great care:

- Not to mislead your employer by stating (or giving the impression) that you have more knowledge, expertise or experience than you actually have!

- To state clearly and assertively that a particular task is outside the boundaries of your professional expertise and experience.

- To be realistic, responsible and proactive in requesting or accessing whatever extra time or resources, advice, help, supervision or training you need to deliver competent performance and to meet agreed deadlines. You may need help from outside the business eg from an independent expert or the relevant professional body.

If you cannot get the time, information, resources or help you need to do the job properly, you may have to refuse to do it – explaining your reasons clearly and carefully to your boss.

Accountants in practice

The concept of **professional competence** and **due care** also applies to individual accountants in practice – you should not accept an assignment that you do not feel competent to work on. In other words, only work on assignments that fall within the confines of your current professional experience, knowledge and expertise.

This principle also applies to the **practice as a whole**. The partners must ensure that they have staff of sufficient skill and expertise to take on a client's engagement, before agreeing to take the client on. If the partners feel that the practice is no longer able to provide a client with sufficient expertise then it should consider withdrawing from the engagement. There are a number of consequences for a practice if it fails to do this.

Breach of contract

The practice will have a **legally binding agreement** (a contract) with each client and this is usually set out in an **engagement letter**.

This letter sets out the terms that the practice agrees to be engaged by the client, for example the type of work to be performed and how the fees are to be calculated.

Whilst the engagement letter might set out the level of expertise that will be offered, the contract will come under section 13 of the **Supply of Goods and Services Act 1982** and this implies a minimum **standard of care** into the agreement.

Under the Act, an accountant must perform their work with **reasonable skill and care**. The level of skill is that of the **reasonable accountant**, although the level may be increased if the accountant is taking on specialised work, or if they profess to have a higher level of skill than the average accountant.

If the client does not receive the level of service that meets this standard then the practice may be taken to court and made to pay **compensation** to the client for any losses they incur as a consequence of the substandard service.

Breach of trust

Accountants are in a **position of trust** with their clients because they hold sensitive information relating to them, possibly hold money on their behalf, and because they hold a high degree of power in the relationship due to being an expert in accountancy matters and the client is not.

This position of trust may be broken if the accountant breaches **client confidentiality** or does not use the client's information for the **benefit of the client**.

In terms of failing to act with sufficient expertise, there may be a breach of trust if the accountant fails to **act in the client's best interest** as a consequence of their lack of expertise. For example, a tax expert would be in breach of trust if they fail to advise the client correctly due to lack of knowledge of tax law and the client ends up paying significantly more tax then they are legally required to.

Like breach of contract, an accountant or a firm that is in breach of trust may be liable to pay the client **compensation**.

Fraud

The **UK Fraud Act 2006**, created three main offences relating to fraud. These are fraud by **false representation** (section 2), fraud by **failing to disclose information** (section 3) and fraud by **abuse of position** (section 4). It is the third offence that we are most concerned with.

A person may be found guilty of **fraud by abuse of position** where they occupy a role where they are expected to safeguard the financial interest of another person, and they dishonestly abuse that position to create a gain for themselves, or causing the other person to suffer a loss. The maximum penalty for this crime is **10 years' imprisonment** and an **unlimited fine**.

Whilst they may not be deliberately behaving dishonestly, an accountant who causes a client to suffer losses, or creates a gain for themselves or their practice, through lack of expertise, is putting themselves at risk of being **accused of fraud**.

Professional negligence

Failing to act with reasonable skill and care may create a liability for the accountant or practice to pay **compensation** to the client or third party for **professional negligence**. Negligence cases are unlike breach of contract or trust in that there does not need to be an agreement between the two parties.

If the accountant performs a service that is **relied upon by another party**, and the work is **defective**, then the accountant may be liable to pay **damages** to the person relying on the work. For this to be the case, there must be some kind of **relationship** between the parties, the accountant must have failed to meet the **standard of care** required of them, and the other party **suffered losses** as a **consequence**.

References and professional negligence

Accountants in practice may be asked by clients or third parties to **provide references**, for example, to provide a reference to a client's bank in support of the client's mortgage application.

To safeguard against the risk of being found liable to pay damages, accountants may add a **disclaimer of liability** to their work. The purpose of a disclaimer of liability is to absolve the accountant from responsibility for any loss or damage suffered by someone else that reads the document and acts upon it.

Examples of such a disclaimer include:

'Whilst every care has been taken in the preparation of this document, it may contain errors for which we cannot be responsible'

or

'This report is prepared for the use of X (the client) only. No responsibility is assumed to any other person.'

The **effectiveness** of such disclaimers is **open to question** by a court. A disclaimer is unlikely to protect the accountant that makes a statement without taking **due care**. It may also **devalue** the report or reference since it gives the impression that the accountant is not confident in the work they have done.

Task 2

Fill in the missing word below.

Section 4 of the Fraud Act 2006 covers fraud by [   ] of position.

POLICIES FOR HANDLING CLIENT MONIES

Accountants who work in practice may come into contact with client monies. **Client monies** are any funds, or form of documents of title to money, or documents of title which can be converted into money that an accountant in practice holds on behalf of a client.

Client monies **do not include** fees for work done or fees paid in advance for work to be done, or the use and control of a client's own bank account. Although, if an accountant has control over the client's own bank account specific written authority must have been obtained and acknowledged by the client's bank. This authority must have been obtained prior to the member exercising control over the account and adequate records of the transactions undertaken must be maintained.

Examples of client monies are:

- Refunds from HMRC received on behalf of a client.

- Funds entrusted to an accountant to assist in carrying out the client's instructions.

- Surplus funds that fall at the end of an engagement.

For example, the practice may be involved in paying a client's suppliers or employees. As a consequence it is important that a number of principles and procedures are followed to avoid threats to a number of fundamental principles.

Handling client monies is also covered in the **ethical code**. The Code states that members in practice must not take custody of their clients' money or other assets unless they are permitted to do so by law.

Why are these rules important? Mishandling client funds may be a **breach of contract** or **professional negligence** if the appropriate standard of care was not followed. Because the client allows the accountant access to their funds in trust, there will be a **breach of trust** if any money is misappropriated.

There is also a risk of being **accused of theft**. The UK Theft Act 1968 defines theft as 'dishonestly appropriating property belonging to another with the intention of permanently depriving the other of it'. For example, transferring client funds to an accountant's own bank account would be theft. An accountant must be careful not to do anything that might be interpreted as theft, it is especially important to be able to demonstrate that the money would be returned to the client at some stage.

Handling clients' money – key safeguards and conditions

Holding client assets can result in self-interest threats to objectivity and professional behaviour. The following are some important safeguards related to **separation, use** and **accountability**.

- **Separation** – clients' monies must be kept separately from monies belonging to the accountant personally and/or to the practice.

- **Use** – clients' monies must be used only for the purpose for which they are intended.

- **Accountability** – accountants must be ready at all times to account for the monies (or any income, dividends or gains generated on them) to the client or authorised enquirers. (failure to do so can result in criminal and/or civil proceedings for theft and/or abuse of position).

The ethical code states that accountants in practice that hold client monies or assets should comply with the laws and regulations relevant to holding and accounting for such assets.

In addition to ensuring the safeguards above are in place, accountants in practice must also ensure:

- Client monies are held in the same currency that they were received in unless the client has given instructions to exchange into another currency.

- The client has been identified and verified on a risk-sensitive basis before holding monies on their behalf.

When not to hold clients' monies

Accountants in practice should not hold clients' monies if:

- They are the monies of investment business clients and you are not regulated.

- There is reason to believe that they are 'criminal property' (obtained from, or to be used for, criminal activities); this would constitute money laundering.

- There is no justification for holding the monies (eg they are not related to a service the member in practice provides).

- There is a condition on your licence or registration that prohibits you from dealing with client monies.

HOW IT WORKS

Franklin Delaney, your new client, phones to ask if you would hold some money on his behalf, 'for reasons he would rather not discuss at the moment'. Although you have carried out due diligence in confirming Mr Delaney's identity and sources of income, you explain to him that you cannot hold any client monies without verifying the commercial purpose of the transaction and the source and destination of the funds.

Meanwhile, another client has deposited funds with you, pending completion on a house purchase; the client will be overseas at the time, and you have agreed to liaise with her solicitor to complete the transaction. It is agreed that your own fees may be drawn from the client account.

CONFIDENTIALITY AND DISCLOSURE

As an accountant, you are likely to have access to a great deal of information about the financial affairs of your clients (or your employers and their clients) that would not, in the normal course of business, be disclosed to the public.

All information you receive through your work as an accountant should be regarded as **confidential**: that is, given in trust (or confidence) that it will not be shared or disclosed.

Confidentiality is one of the fundamental principles of ethics that we looked at in Chapter 1.

Examples include:

- Information shared with the explicit proviso that it be kept **private and confidential**.

- Information shared within a **professional/client relationship** (eg with an accountant or solicitor), which is regarded as a relationship of 'trust and confidence' under the law.

- Information that is **restricted or classified** within an organisation's information system (eg marked 'private', 'confidential' or 'for authorised individuals only').

- Information protected by **data protection and personal privacy law** (eg in the UK, personal data held by organisations, and personal medical data of employees, covered by the **Data Protection Act 1998**).

- Information that could be used **against the interests** of the organisation or an individual.

The Data Protection Act 1998

The **Data Protection Act** gives individuals the right to know what information is held about them. It provides a framework to ensure that personal information is handled properly.

Anyone (an individual or a company) who processes personal information (a **'data controller'**) must be registered to deal with personal information and comply with eight principles, which make sure that personal information is processed correctly and kept secure.

The Act also provides individuals with **important rights**, including the right to find out what personal information is held about them on computer and most paper records.

Should an individual or organisation feel that they are being denied access to personal information, or that their information has not been handled appropriately, they can contact the **Information Commissioner's Office** (ICO). The ICO has legal powers to ensure that organisations comply with the requirements of the Data Protection Act.

Notification is the process by which a data controller gives the ICO details about the processing of personal information. **Notification is a statutory requirement** and every organisation that processes personal information must notify the ICO unless they are exempt. **Failure to notify is a criminal offence.**

The notification period is **one year,** and data controllers must re-register. They must also keep the register up to date, so when any part of the entry becomes inaccurate or incomplete, the ICO must be informed within 28 days. Again failure to do so is a criminal offence.

The principal purpose of having notification and the public register is **transparency** and **openness.** It is a basic principle of data protection that the public should know (or should be able to find out) who is carrying out the processing of personal information as well as other details about the processing (such as for what reason it is being carried out).

Task 3

Fill in the missing number below.

The Information Commissioner's Office (ICO) maintains a public register of data controllers. If any part of a data controller's register becomes inaccurate then they should notify the ICO within [   ] days.

The duty of confidentiality

In Chapter 1 we studied the ethical code in respect of confidentiality, and we will not repeat it here, but you should remember that it states clearly that:

'...members have an obligation to respect the **confidentiality** of information about a client's or employer's affairs, or the affairs of clients of employers, acquired in the course of professional work.'

This may seem obvious, but it extends more widely than you may think:

- It applies even **after the assignment,** or the contractual relationship with the client or employer is over. In other words, you need to respect the confidentiality of information about former clients and ex-employers too.

- It applies not just to you, but to any **staff under your authority**, and any people you ask for advice or assistance. It is up to you to ensure that they keep any information you share with them confidential.

- It applies to the **use of information**, not just disclosure. It is a breach of confidentiality to use confidential information to your advantage, even if you do not disclose it to anyone.

When *can* you disclose confidential information?

As we saw earlier, disclosure of confidential information is a difficult and complex area and members are therefore sometimes specifically advised to seek professional advice before disclosing it.

You are permitted to disclose confidential information in three specific sets of circumstances:

(1) **When you are properly authorised to do so and this is permitted by law**

The client or employer may legitimately authorise you to disclose the information. However, you still need to consider the effect of disclosure; will it be in the best interests of all the parties involved in the matter?

(2) **When you have a professional duty or right to do so, which is in the public interest and is not prohibited by law**

You are entitled to disclose information if it is necessary to do so in order to perform your work properly, according to the technical standards and ethical requirements of the profession.

You also have a duty to disclose information if asked to do so by a professional or other regulatory body, as part of an ethical or disciplinary investigation into your conduct (or the conduct of your employer or client).

Another example is to protect the member's professional interests in legal proceedings.

(3) **When you have a legal duty to do so**

UK law requires you to:

(a) Produce documents or give evidence if asked to do so by a court of law, in the course of **legal proceedings** against you, or your client or employer.

(b) Disclose certain information to bodies that have **statutory powers** to demand the information, such as **HMRC**.

(c) Disclose certain **illegal activities** to appropriate public authorities. Not all illegal activities must be reported in this way; there may be other regulatory machinery for dealing with them. However, some activities are covered by specific legal provisions, particularly in relation to public safety, organised crime, money laundering and terrorism.

HOW IT WORKS

Your in-tray this morning contains three requests for information:

- You receive a formal demand from HMRC for information regarding the VAT returns of a client.

  You report this to one of the partners, who says he will refer the matter to the firm's legal advisers.

- A property developer, who is a client of yours, has written asking whether you know of any businesses in the city looking to sell a commercial property.

  You recall that a petrol station client of yours has told you that they are intending to sell. However, you are also aware that the value of the property (for its current purposes) will fall once a scheme for a new by-pass is announced. Both these facts are covered by client confidentiality.

  You call the petrol station owners and ask them if you can disclose their plans to the property developer. They give permission, so you pass the message to the developer. At the same time, you advise him of the need to carry out 'due diligence' for any purchase, including checking any development applications already under consideration by the Town Planners – without suggesting any specific reason to do so.

You follow up with a letter to both the petrol station owners and the property developers, recommending that they seek independent advice regarding the sale/purchase; this enables you to avoid taking on a conflict of interest between the two clients (if one wins and one loses from the transaction).

- A new employee has given you her banking details, for payroll. She has also included some information about the rates of pay and benefits paid by her previous employer, and some of its payroll practices – apparently just to explain how delighted she is by the generosity and integrity of your company.

This data may have been given in good faith – but it is inappropriate to disclose confidential details of a previous employer. You delete the email, having recorded the relevant banking details. You also make a note to have a quiet word with her about confidentiality.

Factors to consider in disclosing information

Even if the information can legitimately be disclosed, you still have to consider a number of points in deciding whether or how to proceed:

- **How reliable is the information?** If all the relevant facts are known and supported by good evidence, the disclosure may be clear cut – but if all you have is unsupported facts, opinions or suspicions, you may have to use your professional judgement as to whether you disclose, how and to whom.

- **Who is the appropriate recipient of the information?** You need to be sure that the person to whom you give the information is the right person; in other words, they have a legitimate right to it, and the authority to act on it.

- **Will you incur legal liability by disclosing the information?** Some disclosures (such as reporting money laundering) are legally 'privileged' and you cannot be sued for breach of professional confidentiality. This is as long as the disclosure is made in good faith and with reasonable grounds. Other situations may not be so clear cut and you may need to consider getting advice from a solicitor before proceeding with a disclosure without the client's authorisation.

- **How can you protect the on-going confidentiality of the information as far as possible?** If you make a disclosure, you have a responsibility to ensure that it is made only to the relevant parties, and that they understand their responsibilities to protect the information from further disclosure. At least, ensure that you send the information direct to the relevant party, clearly labelled 'confidential' or 'for your eyes only'.

In Chapter 4, we will look at the specific case of disclosure of information by an employee of illegal or unethical practices by his or her employer – this is known as whistle blowing.

Task 4

In which of the following circumstances would you be permitted to disclose confidential information about a client or your employer?

	✓
When your client or employer authorises you.	
When HMRC requires you to.	
When a court requires you to do so.	

CHAPTER OVERVIEW

- An accountant has a professional duty to maintain an **appropriate professional distance** (independence) between their work and their personal life at all times.

- There is a self-interest threat if members in business, or their close or personal relations or associates have **a financial interest** in their employing organisation.

- **Gifts and hospitality** or **inducements** can also pose self-interest and intimidation threats to an accountant's objectivity and confidentiality.

- Potential threats to the principle of **competence and due care** include: time pressure (when there may not be enough time to complete a task properly); insufficient or inaccurate information; lack of resources (eg equipment or help); or your own lack of experience, knowledge or training.

- Accountants in practice face a number of consequences for failing to act with sufficient expertise, such as **breach of contract**, **breach of trust**, **accusations of fraud** and **professional negligence**.

- Key principles in handling or **holding clients' monies** are separation, dedicated use and accountability.

- All information you receive through your work as an accountant should be regarded as **confidential**.

- The **Data Protection Act** gives individuals the right to know what information is held about them. It provides a framework to ensure that personal information is handled properly.

- You are permitted to disclose confidential information in three specific sets of circumstances: when you are properly **authorised** to do so; when you have a **professional** duty to do so; when you have a **legal** duty to do so.

TEST YOUR LEARNING

Respond to the following by selecting the appropriate option.

Test 1

Accepting gifts or hospitality from a client can give rise to which of the following threats to an accountant's fundamental principles?

	✓
Self-interest	
Self-review	
Advocacy	
Familiarity	

Test 2

Being bribed [▼] an offence under the Bribery Act 2010.

Picklist:

is
is not

Test 3

An accountant in practice can keep client monies together with monies belonging to them personally, or the practice, as long as they have the client's permission.

	✓
True	
False	

Test 4

Notification to the Information Commissioner's Office by data controllers about the processing of personal information is a statutory requirement, and failing to do so is a criminal offence.

	✓
True	
False	

Test 5

Your duty of confidentiality to a client or employer continues even after your contractual relationship with them has ended.

	✓
True	
False	

BPP
LEARNING MEDIA

chapter 4:
TAKING APPROPRIATE ACTION

chapter coverage 📖

Unfortunately, ethical issues are seldom clear-cut. You may often encounter situations where a course of action appears to be on the 'borderline' between ethical (or at least widely accepted) and unethical.

How do you know which is the 'right' course of action in a given situation or interaction? This chapter offers some guidance.

The topics covered are:

✍ Identifying appropriate ethical behaviours

✍ Money laundering

✍ Taxation services

✍ Conflicting loyalties

✍ Dealing with ethical conflicts

✍ Dealing with illegal or unethical conduct by an employer

✍ Dealing with inappropriate client behaviour

✍ Whistle blowing

IDENTIFYING APPROPRIATE ETHICAL BEHAVIOURS

Ethics and the law

To be ethical, conduct must also be legal. You need to comply with the law, encourage your colleagues and employers (where relevant) to comply with the law – and advise your clients to comply with the law.

You may have encountered a range of legal issues in your personal life or workplace; be aware that these are all potentially relevant to professional ethics, insofar as they affect your behaviour and reputation as an accountant.

You must remember that the conceptual framework for dealing with ethical dilemmas takes precedence in your professional work. Consider the ethical principles at risk, identify threats, implement safeguards using your professional judgement and if the threats cannot be eliminated or reduced to a sufficiently low level you should resign or withdraw from the assignment.

Task 1

Give five examples of laws that affect (or should affect) your everyday behaviour at work – not necessarily in the way you perform your accounting duties.

Critical decision-making on ethical issues

When considering what to do about an ethical issue, first of all, consider the application of available **legal** and **ethical guidelines** in the particular situation you are facing:

- How might the principles apply?
- Are there examples (or legal precedents) that might act as a template?

If the situation is still unclear, critical decision-making may be required. Two sets of ideas may be useful in helping you to reach a reasoned conclusion that will withstand later scrutiny:

- **Consider the consequences.** What will be the effects of the course of action – on you and others? An action may have both positive and negative impacts, or may affect some people positively and others negatively. However, a course of action that is likely to have an unacceptably high cost for any of the parties concerned may be said to be unethical.

  A **basic test** is to consider whether you would feel comfortable and confident, if you had to defend your decision or action before a court, or in the press, or to a moral/spiritual adviser you admire?

If not, this may be an indication that, deep down, you know that it is potentially unethical.

- **Consider your obligations**. What do you 'owe' other people in the situation? Some obligations are clearly set out in contracts (eg with employers and clients) – but we also, arguably, have a general 'duty' to treat others fairly and humanely.

    A **basic test** (using the 'golden rule', which is part of all major ethical systems) is to consider: would you want to be on the receiving end of whatever action you are about to take? If not, this may be an indication that it is potentially unethical.

So the **key questions** are:

(a) Is it legal and in line with company policy and professional guidelines?
(b) How will it make me feel about myself?
(c) Is it balanced and fair to all concerned?

There are also outside sources of advice and guidance, which you may choose to access – but it is important to observe the requirement for **confidentiality** until you are sure that the situation is such that you have a right and duty to disclose it.

Decision-making in business ethics

To help develop ethical business cultures, the **Institute of Business Ethics** (IBE) was established with the aim of encouraging high standards of business behaviour based on ethical values.

The IBE's website contains a lot of information on the purpose of ethics policies and programmes and also how to develop a code of ethics and make it work within an organisation.

The IBE also sets out the simple ethical tests for a business decision. Some companies provide their employees with ethical tests to help them make decisions, ie a series of questions to ask themselves. The IBE's simple ethical tests for a business decision are:

- **Transparency** ('Do I mind others knowing what I have decided?')
- **Effect** ('Who does my decision affect or hurt?')
- **Fairness** ('Would my decision be considered fair by those affected?')

Getting help with ethical concerns and dealing with malpractice

If you are employed by an organisation, any matter of ethical concern, or of a colleague's malpractice – whether or not it is explicitly addressed in the ethical code for accountants – should be raised with your immediate supervisor, or employee helpline, if available.

However, if the ethical issue concerns the organisation, or if you are self-employed, you may need to seek independent advice – within the requirements for professional confidentiality:

- Seek **independent legal advice** (particularly if there are potential legal consequences to your actions). Legal advisers are also bound by professional confidentiality, so this offers protection to you and the others involved in the situation. (Talking to a spouse or partner, friend or colleague does not!)

- If you are still in doubt about the proper course of action, you can contact the ethics helpline of your professional body.

Written records should be kept of any such discussions and meetings (as for other forms of conflict resolution at work), to ensure that there is evidence of the advice you have received. This will help protect you in any legal proceedings that may result.

HOW IT WORKS

At your firm of Chartered Accountants, you have been asked by the partner to whom you report to sit in and take notes as she interviews an applicant for the post of receptionist with the firm. In the course of the interview, your attention is drawn to the following aspects of the discussion:

- The partner, having learned that the candidate has three small children, asks lots of questions about her plans to have more children and her childcare arrangements. When the candidate, in return, asks about the firm's family-friendly working policies, you notice that the partner omits to mention the childcare assistance that you know is available.

- The candidate reveals that the family depends mainly on income from her husband's job at a local electrical goods manufacturer. As it happens, this company is one of your clients – and you are aware of its plans to shut down the local plant over the coming year.

- The candidate left her previous employers because they continued to employ a successful member of their sales staff who had sexually harassed her and another female employee. This firm is another client of your firm.

After the candidate has left, the partner looks across at you and rolls her eyes and says, 'Just lose those notes, will you?'.

What are the ethical issues raised here, and how will you decide what (if anything) to do about them?

- The partner's focus on family responsibilities may be construed as sexual discrimination under UK law – unless she asks the same questions of any men she interviews for the job.

- Giving incomplete information about the organisation might be more significantly unethical if its effect was to mislead someone into taking employment under false pretences. In this case, not much harm is being done, as the candidate is merely being influenced against accepting a job that she probably will not be offered.

- You may feel sorry for the family, who are unaware that the husband will soon lose his job. But this is a fact of economic life – and you have the overriding duty of confidentiality not to disclose what you know about the client's plans.

- The behaviour of the candidate's previous employer is unethical. But you have come by the information indirectly – and is it anything to do with you? It would certainly be in your client's best interests not to risk legal claims against them.

- The partner's request to you to 'lose' the notes is ambiguous. It sounds unethical – whether as a suggestion of prejudice against the candidate, or as a way of dodging responsibility for the ethical issues raised.

So what might you do? First you might decide to clarify exactly what the partner meant; this would clear up any misunderstanding, and highlight the ethical issues more clearly. It might also be possible to draw her attention (respectfully) to the risks of her interview questions being construed as discrimination.

Other than this, it may not be your place to do much more – although you may choose to advise your clients of the ethical and legal considerations that have come to your attention: the need to be socially responsible in notifying employees as early as possible of impending redundancies; and the need for consistency, fairness and compliance with regard to disciplinary issues (such as sexual harassment).

MONEY LAUNDERING

A key example of the need to take appropriate action over illegal or unethical activities is the case of **money laundering**. We have mentioned money laundering already in this chapter when we discussed the provision of taxation services, as well as in earlier chapters in various contexts. In this section, we look at money laundering in more detail.

The AAT's Appendix to Unit Guidance for PETH provides detailed information on money laundering and you should refer to it if you need to (it is reproduced in the front pages of this Text). **Assessment questions may be set on the information contained within the appendix.**

We have already mentioned the pieces of legislation that form part of the UK anti-money laundering legislation. To recap, these are:

- The Proceeds of Crime Act 2002 (POCA)
- The Terrorism Act 2000 (TA)
- The Money Laundering Regulations 2007

Money laundering is statutorily defined as an act which constitutes an offence under sections 327, 328 and 329 of the Proceeds of Crime Act. These are:

- Concealing, disguising, converting, transferring or removing criminal property (section 327).

- Taking part in an arrangement to facilitate the acquisition, use or control of criminal property (section 328).

- Acquiring, using or possessing criminal property (section 329).

Terrorism is defined as the use or threat of action designed to influence government, or to intimidate any section of the public, or to advance a political, religious or ideological cause where the action would involve violence, threats to health and safety, damage to property or disruption of electronic systems.

Importantly, there are **no de minimis** exceptions in relation to either money laundering or terrorist financing offences. This means there are no minimum limits to which offences relating to money laundering or terrorist financing can be applied. Thus, all offences which result in proceeds, however trivial, must be reported.

There can be no hard and fast rules on how to recognise it, but money laundering is generally defined as **the process by which the proceeds of crime, and the true ownership of those proceeds, are changed so that the proceeds appear to come from a legitimate source**. In UK law, it is an offence to obtain, conceal or invest funds or property, if you know or suspect that they are the proceeds of criminal conduct or terrorist funding ('criminal property').

The **maximum period of imprisonment** that can be imposed on a person found guilty of money laundering or terrorist financing is **14 years**. An **unlimited fine** may also be imposed.

You may think that you are unlikely to come across criminal property – but it is not all about the kinds of crime you see on TV cop shows! It includes the proceeds of tax evasion, benefits obtained through bribery and corruption, and benefits (eg saved costs) arising from a failure to comply with a regulatory requirement (eg cutting corners on health and safety provisions). Because there is no de minimis exception, even small amounts are included in the definition.

Financial institutions and non-financial businesses and professions are required to adopt **specific measures** to help identify and prevent money laundering and terrorist financing.

These include:

- Implementing client checking (customer due diligence), record-keeping and internal suspicion-reporting measures. This includes the appointment of a **Money Laundering Reporting Officer (MLRO)**.

- Not doing or disclosing anything that might prejudice an investigation into such activities. This specifically includes any word or action that might '**tip off**' the money launderers that they are, or may come, under investigation. You are, however, entitled to advise clients on issues regarding prevention of money laundering on a non-specific basis. We look at the penalties for tipping off later in the chapter.

- **Disclosing** any knowledge or suspicion of money laundering activity to the appropriate authorities. It is specifically stated that **accounting professionals** will not be in breach of their professional duty of confidentiality (and therefore cannot be sued) if they report, in good faith, any knowledge or suspicions in relation to money laundering to the appropriate authority.

There are also requirements to be followed on record keeping under the **Money Laundering Regulations 2007**. These state that records should be kept to assist in any future legal investigations and to show that the accountant has followed statutory requirements.

Customer due diligence identification evidence should be kept for **five years** from the date when the accountant's relationship with the client ends.

Customer due diligence information on transactions should be kept for **five years** from the date when the accountant completed the client's instructions.

Proceeds of Crime Act 2002

The **Proceeds of Crime Act 2002** created a single set of money laundering offences applicable throughout the UK to the proceeds of all crimes. It also created a disclosure regime, which makes it an offence for an accountant as part of the regulated sector (see below) not to disclose knowledge or suspicion of money laundering. The activities embraced by the definition of money laundering offences in the legislation include even passive possession of criminal property as money laundering.

POCA established a number of money laundering offences including:

- Principal **money laundering** offences (see above).

- Offences of **failing to report** suspected money laundering.

- Offences of **tipping off** about a money laundering disclosure or investigation, and **prejudicing money laundering investigations**.

Who must disclose?

People who work in the **regulated sector** are those who provide specified professional services such as accountancy. This therefore includes accountants in practice.

'Relevant persons' are sole traders and firms (not employees) who operate within the regulated sector. Relevant persons have a duty to establish and maintain practice, policies and procedures (ie customer due diligence, reporting and record keeping) to detect and deter money laundering and terrorist financing.

When to disclose?

Under the Proceeds of Crime Act and Terrorism Act, accountants (including AAT members in practice) have a **duty to report** knowledge or suspicion about money laundering or terrorist financing when:

- The accountant knows or has reasonable grounds to suspect that another person is engaged in money laundering or terrorist financing, whether or not he or she wishes to act for such a person or

- The accountant wishes to provide services in relation to property which he or she knows or suspects relates to money laundering or terrorist financing. If this is the case, the reporter must indicate in the report that consent is required to provide such services, and must refrain from doing so until consent is received.

If the accountant suspects another person is engaged in money laundering or terrorist financing, that person may be a client, a colleague or a third party.

There are, however, some **exceptions to the duty to report**.

The obligation to report does not apply if the basis of the knowledge or suspicion was not obtained in the accountant's normal course of business. For example a disclosure is not required if the information was obtained at a social event outside of work.

There is also no duty to report if the information was obtained in privileged circumstances (eg so the accountant could provide legal advice), or if there is a reasonable excuse for not reporting (as long as the report is made as soon as is reasonable in the circumstances).

How to disclose?

If there is an obligation to make a report (a disclosure), the accountant must submit:

- An **Internal Report to a Money Laundering Reporting Officer (MLRO)**, if they are employed in a group practice.

- A **Suspicious Activity Report (SAR)** to the National Crime Agency (NCA), if they are a sole practitioner or an MLRO.

A person commits an offence if he/she fails to disclose this knowledge or suspicion, or reasonable grounds for suspicion, as soon as practicable to a nominated officer (MLRO) if working in a firm, or NCA, if working as a sole practitioner. The maximum **penalty for failure to disclose** is **five years** in prison or an **unlimited fine**.

The following information forms part of the **required disclosure**

- Identity of the suspect (if known)
- The information on which the knowledge or suspicion is based
- Whereabouts of the laundered property (if known)

Reports made under the Proceeds of Crime Act

A report made under the Proceeds of Crime Act is either:

- A protected disclosure
- An authorised disclosure

'Protected' disclosures are made by someone who knows or suspects another of money laundering. Making the required disclosure in the appropriate way means the person making the disclosure is protected against allegations of breach of confidentiality.

An **'authorised' disclosure** is made by the money launderer themselves and should be made by a person who realises they may have or may be about to engage in money laundering, An authorised disclosure may provide a defence against charges of money laundering if it is made before the act is carried out or as soon as possible afterwards, provided there is a good reason for the delay. A good reason might be that at the time of the act the person didn't realise criminal property was involved.

Any person can make an authorised or protected disclosure. However, **protected disclosures are compulsory in the regulated sector**.

Members in business should therefore make an authorised disclosure if they are personally involved in an act which might constitute money laundering, and they should encourage their employer to make a disclosure, but they are not required to as they are not in the regulated sector.

Tipping off

After the required disclosure has been submitted in either an internal report to an MLRO, or an SAR to NCA, even if the accountant did not submit the report but still knows about it or suspects a report has been made, the accountant must not subsequently disclose any information likely to prejudice any investigation. In most cases this means the accountant should not tell the suspect about either the report or the investigation.

If the accountant does make such a disclosure they are committing the criminal offence of 'tipping off'. The offence can apply even if it was not the accountant's intention to prejudice an investigation. Note that the tipping off offence only applies to relevant persons in the regulated sector.

The maximum penalty for this tipping off offence for accountants is **five years imprisonment or an unlimited fine**.

Prejudicing an investigation

There is also an offence that may be committed by **any person** (not just an accountant). This 'prejudicing an investigation' offence occurs when any person:

- Knows or suspects that a money laundering investigation is being (or is about to be) conducted; and

- Makes a disclosure which is likely to prejudice the investigation; or

- Falsifies, conceals or destroys documents relevant to the investigation, or causes that to happen.

As with tipping off, the 'prejudicing an investigation' offence can still apply if the person did not intend to prejudice an investigation when making the disclosure. However, there is a defence available if the person making the disclosure did not know or suspect the disclosure would be prejudicial, did not know or suspect the documents were relevant, or did not intend to conceal any facts from the person carrying out the investigation.

HOW IT WORKS

When you visited your client's café business recently, you noticed that they had employed an additional chef – but now, checking the payroll reports, you cannot find any mention of this person, or any payments made to her.

You would like to check that your suspicions (that the employee is being paid cash so they and the employer avoid tax liabilities) are well-founded, but you are aware of the danger of '**tipping off**' the client.

This type of activity is known as concealing a tax liability, because funds which are rightfully HMRC's are being retained by the business and the employee, and it is a form of money laundering.

As a relevant person in a regulated sector you may have to make a protected report to your MLRO, although the internal rules of your practice may mean you should report it to the partner in charge of the client before doing so.

Task 2

Fill in the missing number below.

The maximum penalty for being found guilty of money laundering is [   ] years in prison.

TAXATION SERVICES

Much of the work firms of accountants do for individuals and companies concerns the preparation of tax returns and supplying tax advice. This can present the accountant with ethical dilemmas because clients want to minimise the amount of tax they pay, but the law requires the accountant to ensure they pay the amount of tax required by legislation.

Codes of ethics for accountants provide general guidance on taxation issues, however some guidance is dependant on the jurisdiction that the accountant is working in. For example, the AAT Code is dependent on UK law in relation to the disclosure of tax errors.

The AAT Code states that accountants providing taxation services have a duty to put the **best interest of the client** forward, but this must be done **legally** and with regard to the fundamental principles of **integrity, objectivity and professional competence**. To this end, accountants must ensure that clients are aware of the **limitations** attached to taxation advice so that they do not misinterpret an expression of opinion as an assertion of fact.

Accountants must only perform taxation work on the basis of **full disclosure** by clients – it is the client who is responsible for the accuracy of facts, information and computations provided to the member.

Where accountants submit tax returns or tax computations for a client, they are acting as **agents** of the client. The respective responsibilities of accountant and client must be clearly set out in the **letter of engagement**.

Where accountants in practice are acting for a tax client, they must provide **copies** of all computations to the client **before** submitting them to HMRC.

Accountants should take care not to associate themselves with a tax return or related communication if they have any reason to believe that it is **false** or **misleading** eg:

- If it contains a false or misleading statement.

- If it leaves out or obscures information that should be submitted, in such a way as to mislead the tax authorities.

- If it contains statements or information that have been provided carelessly, without the taxpayer checking or knowing whether they are true or false (and therefore being potentially false or misleading).

Tax errors and omissions are specifically mentioned in the study and assessment guide for this unit. If an accountant finds out about a **material error or omission** in a tax return from a prior year, or of **failure to file a tax return**, they must carry out the following:

- Advise the client or employer promptly about the error or omission.

- Recommend the client or employer to make disclosure to HMRC.

- If the client or employer does not correct the error, inform them in writing that they cannot continue to act as their accountant.

- Accountants in practice should report the client's refusal to the MLRO in the firm or to NCA (if a sole practitioner), without disclosing this to anyone.

- Accountants in business should report the refusal and surrounding facts to NCA if they have acted in relation to the error or omission. If they have not themselves acted, they are not obliged to report the matter, though making a report in the appropriate manner will not amount to a breach of confidentiality.

You should also note that for the purposes of the money laundering provisions, the proceeds of **deliberate tax evasion** – including under-declaring income and over-claiming expenses – are just as much 'criminal property' as money from drug trafficking, terrorist activity or theft. You therefore have a duty to report the client's or employer's activities to the relevant authority (such as the MLRO or NCA in the UK).

Particular ethical issues are raised by performing taxation services (preparing tax returns, giving tax advice and so on), since there is a complex administrative and legal framework for both direct taxation (based on income, gains, profits and losses) and indirect taxation (such as VAT).

The **AAT's sponsoring bodies** that deal with taxation and the **Chartered Institute of Taxation**, have extensive ethical guidelines in this area. Key issues are **integrity, professional competence** and **confidentiality**.

Task 3

What should you do if a client asks you how much tax you will be able to save them this year?

	✓
Provide them with a reasonable estimate based on what you achieved last year.	
Tell them that you will save them as much as possible.	
Tell them that you cannot provide such information.	

Task 4

What should you do if you become aware of a significant error in a tax return that you prepared and submitted for a client in a previous year?

	✓
Do nothing as admitting errors will damage your professional reputation.	
Correct the error by adjusting this year's tax return to compensate.	
Tell the client to advise HMRC about the error.	

A final thing to note relevant to ethical reporting in relation to taxation services is that **HM Revenue & Customs (HMRC)** has extensive legal powers to obtain information that may otherwise be withheld. If a statutory demand for information is made by HMRC, you should comply in line with the guidelines on breaching confidentiality that we saw in Chapter 1, possibly after seeking legal advice.

HOW IT WORKS

You are concerned about one your clients, a catering business. Although you are satisfied that personal expenditures of the owners have not been included in the financial statements of the business, you have not had an adequate response to a query you raised about undeclared income in its office catering arm.

The owners supply you with a general assurance, in writing, that all income is being declared. However, you have lingering doubts. The business is not reducing its purchases of supplies, nor the hours of its delivery staff – yet recorded sales are still very low when compared with comparable periods in previous years. At the same time, you note that mobile phone costs of all staff are being claimed as business expenses, on the grounds of 'extensive off-site trading'.

It is now time to prepare the client's tax return.

Having discussed the matter with one of your firm's partners, you meet with the client to ensure that they understand that they are responsible for making full and accurate disclosure to the tax authorities, and are prepared to sign a statement to this effect. They reply that, as they see it, you are supposed to be 'on their side' to save them tax. You explain your professional and legal obligations and emphasise that you cannot knowingly associate yourself with a misleading return. As long as you have reason to believe that there may be errors or omissions, you will not be able to act for them in preparing or submitting this return.

CONFLICTING LOYALTIES

If you are an employed member of a professional body, or an accountant in business, you owe a **duty of loyalty** to your employer, to your profession and to the public interest.

Where does your duty lie?

As an employee, your first duty will generally be to contribute to your organisation's objectives (ends), and to comply with all reasonable instructions, requests, rules and procedures (means) designed to further them.

But what if some of these ends or means are unethical (as defined by the standards of your profession)? Where does your primary duty lie?

Your employer cannot **legitimately** require you to:

- Break the law.

- Break the rules and standards of the accounting profession.

- Put your name to, or otherwise be associated with, a statement which significantly misrepresents facts (particularly in connection with financial statements, tax or legal compliance).

- Lie to or mislead regulators or the firm's internal or external auditors.

- Facilitate, or be part of, the handling of unethical or illegal earnings (ie money laundering).

The law and rules and standards of your profession take clear priority in such a conflict of loyalties: your duty is to refuse to obey the instruction or rule, unless it can be shown that it is not, after all, incompatible with legal and professional requirements.

This may be easier said than done, particularly if you are a junior employee and are being put under pressure by an influential (or personally overbearing) superior. You may need all your assertive communication techniques!

At the same time, it is worth remembering that not every difference of opinion on ethical issues is an ethical conflict – and not every ethical conflict is significant enough to present a real conflict of loyalties. In other words, pick your battles wisely!

DEALING WITH ETHICAL CONFLICTS

The ethical code sets out some advice to accountants in business concerning how ethical conflicts should be dealt with. It basically states that they have a duty to comply with the fundamental principles. However, there may be situations where their work responsibilities clash the fundamental principles. Where this happens, and compliance with the fundamental principles is under threat, accountants have to assess the threats and apply safeguards to eliminate them or reduce them to an acceptable level.

Safeguards could include:

- Obtaining advice from within their employing organisation, an independent adviser or a professional body.

- Using a formal dispute resolution process within the employing organisation.

- Seeking legal advice.

What is an ethical conflict?

It is almost inevitable that at some time in your career, you will meet a situation that presents some kind of ethical dilemma or conflict, where:

- Two ethical **values or requirements** seem to be incompatible, eg you have the duty to disclose unethical conduct that has come to your attention – but also the duty of professional confidentiality.

- Two sets of **demands and obligations** seem to be incompatible (conflicting loyalties), eg if an employer or client asks you to break the ethical guidelines of your profession by: falsifying a record; making a misleading statement; or supplying information 'recklessly', without being in a position to know whether or not it is true.

  Such situations may be particularly acute if you are put under pressure to do the wrong thing by an overbearing supervisor, or by a valued client, friend or relation.

Note that not everyone thinks alike on all ethical matters. It is quite possible that a fellow professional, or a work colleague, will honestly disagree with you about what constitutes an ethical or unethical course of action; this does not necessarily mean that you have an 'ethical conflict', or that you have to report and formally resolve the matter.

The kind of genuine ethical conflict that must be resolved is one that puts you in a position where you are being asked or required to take – or be party to – action that you feel may be unethical or that means you are not complying with the fundamental principles.

Resolving ethical conflicts

The AAT Code provides an example of a structure for resolving ethical conflicts.

If you are asked, instructed or encouraged to take a course of action that is illegal, or unethical by the standards of your profession, you are entitled and required to refuse.

This can lead to interpersonal – and perhaps even legal – conflict.

Some issues may be 'cleared up' by **informal discussion**; they may be based on a misunderstanding, or ignorance – or the belief that no-one knows what is going on! Your first aim will be to persuade the relevant parties not to take (or persist in) the unethical course of action.

If informal discussion does not work, and the issue is significant, more **formal** avenues may be pursued.

Whether informal or formal routes are taken, the member must consider the following factors:

- Relevant facts
- Ethical issues involved
- Fundamental principles
- Established internal procedures
- Alternative courses of action

Once the member has considered these factors, they should think about courses of action that are consistent with the fundamental principles. It is also important for the member to consider the consequences of each course of action.

Within an organisation there may be **established procedures** for resolving ethical issues and conflicts with colleagues or superiors, such as those for dealing with grievances. If this does not produce a satisfactory result, the problem should be discussed with the next level up in the management hierarchy, and/or arbitrators such as an Ethics Committee or ethics partner, or other senior members of staff.

The member may consider consulting those involved in the governance of the organisation, such as the board of directors or the audit committee. Whether such consultation is needed, and which persons are most appropriate to consult, will be determined by the specific circumstances in which the member finds themselves in. The member may find advice in their organisation's internal procedures or from a professional adviser.

The Code of Professional Ethics provides some guidance on the matter. It states that if such communications are made, the member should consider the nature and importance of the particular circumstances and matter to be communicated, and the appropriate person(s) within the entity's governance structure with whom to communicate.

It goes on to say that if the member communicates with a subgroup of those charged with governance – for example, an audit committee or an individual – the member or firm shall determine whether communication with all of those charged with governance is also necessary so that they are adequately informed.

If a conflict still exists after all internal avenues to resolution have been explored, the accountant may have no alternative but to resign.

For an accountant in practice, if a client requests or instructs you to take a course of action that is unethical or illegal, you are entitled and required to refuse. The request may be made in ignorance and good faith – and you should attempt to explain the technical, legal and ethical principles that apply. If the client continues to insist, or refuses to change his or her own unethical conduct (where this reflects on you as his or her agent or adviser), you should simply cease to act for that client.

At all times during the resolution process it is important to document the issue together with any discussions held or decisions taken in connection with it. This is in case you are required to show your professional body that you took the matter seriously and how you dealt with it. This may be some time after the event so it is important to keep a record at the time. It may also be required in legal proceedings if the matter is taken that far.

If you have difficulty in resolving the conflict you could consider taking advice from your professional body or a legal advisor. Where advice is given to you on a confidential basis you would not be in breach of the principle of confidentiality. You might use such advice where, for example, you think a client might be money laundering and need advice to decide whether or not you think your suspicions are justified.

If the issue is unresolved, even if you have taken steps to protect your own integrity and reputation by resigning or ceasing to act, you may still have a duty to report illegal conduct to relevant authorities. This is a tricky area, because of the competing duty of confidentiality.

HOW IT WORKS

You have some concerns regarding inaccuracies in the amounts of time some of your colleagues in practice charge their clients which often result in clients paying for an accountant's time which has not been spent on the client's work. When you report this to the partner she says 'Forget it, the clients are still getting good value for money one way or another. Do you think the partners waste time tying down every hour that goes astray here or there? You worry too much'.

There will be an ethical conflict if you choose to pursue the matter (as compromising your professional ethics) and the partner insists that you let the matter drop. The culture of your firm, from the top down, is clearly unsympathetic to what are seen as 'minor' ethical concerns. You may have to go to the Ethics Committee (which should include impartial members), or get independent advice as to whether or how to take the matter further.

Meanwhile, you have sat in on another interview for the post of receptionist. This candidate, who is very keen and is currently working for another firm of chartered accountants in the city, appears to be the perfect person for the job. As the partner is bringing the interview to a close, the candidate says: 'By the way, I thought you might like to see the kind of systems I've got experience with. Here's a copy, on disk, of our Contacts Management software.'

After the interview, you tell the partner that you are not comfortable about this. She says that although it is, technically, a breach of copyright, she will destroy the disk after looking over it; this is probably within the definition of 'fair dealing'.

You suspect, however, that the candidate has actually handed her a competing firm's (highly confidential) client/contact list. This would clearly be unethical to accept, let alone use. Does the partner have similar suspicions, or is she acting in ignorance? Did the candidate offer the disk in good faith – or as an incentive to influence the selection decision? You should state your concerns clearly about this. If the partner knowingly takes advantage of unethically-obtained information, and expects you to be silent about it, you are being made party to an unethical course of action; this is a serious ethical conflict, and you should get confidential independent advice on how to deal with it.

DEALING WITH ILLEGAL OR UNETHICAL CONDUCT BY AN EMPLOYER

In addition to ethical conflicts directly affecting your own work, you may become aware that your employer has committed (or may be about to commit) an act that you believe to be illegal or unethical.

Examples include:

- Various forms of **fraud**.

- **Falsification of records**, or the supply of information or statements that are false or misleading.

- The **offer of inducements** to influence external parties (such as government officials) who have power to help or hinder the employer's operations. This may take the form of bribes (payments made to secure services to which a company is not legally entitled) or 'grease money' (payments made to speed up services that are being stalled or obstructed). 'Gifts' are more problematical (particularly in some cultures, where they are regarded as part of civilised negotiation), but they are unethical if their intent is to influence decisions in the company's favour (eg to win a contract).

- The **acceptance of inducements** to help or hinder the interests of others, or to compromise objectivity and impartiality. For example, clients may offer inducements to collude in fraud or money-laundering, to overlook financial irregularities and so on.

- Other **illegal activity** – from health and safety violations, to money-laundering, to breach of copyright, sexual discrimination or misuse of personal data.

Your aim in dealing with such a situation is, initially, to persuade your employer not to initiate or complete the act, or to put things right and/or to change its policies and controls to ensure that the problem does not occur again.

There may be specific machinery to facilitate this process, or you may have to report the matter to successive levels of management with the power of decision-making in relevant areas.

There may be an Ethics Committee in the organisation: a group of executives (perhaps including non-executive directors) appointed to oversee company ethics and to make rulings on allegations of misconduct.

HOW IT WORKS

A payroll clerk at your company approaches you and asks if you can give her some personal advice. You say that you will try to help – if you can – on the understanding that you cannot take responsibility.

It appears that the production department has been tipped off that a Health and Safety Inspector will be visiting the factory in a couple of days, following a complaint. Apparently, the factory supervisors are busy replacing safety guards on machinery, and covering up torn flooring – and generally disguising potential safety hazards.

Now the production manager has asked the payroll clerk for a management report on sickness and injury pay, but the specific parameters he has set for the information will make it look as if there have been fewer and less serious accidents than has in fact been the case.

At this point, you stop the clerk and say that it would be inappropriate for you to hear more, but in your opinion this may be a genuine ethical conflict (if all the facts are true), as she is apparently being asked knowingly to present a misleading report. You advise her to speak in the first instance to her own supervisor, stating her concerns and asking the supervisor to take the matter up with the production manager.

DEALING WITH INAPPROPRIATE CLIENT BEHAVIOUR

We have already seen how an accountant should deal with illegal client behaviour, in relation to money laundering and prejudicing an investigation, so we now turn our attention to inappropriate behaviour. This is behaviour which is not necessarily illegal, but puts the accountant at risk of breaching their ethical principles. **Inappropriate behaviour by a client** can be classified into three groups, in relation to the type of threat that they present to ethical principles.

Familiarity threat

As you know, familiarity threats are often created by not maintaining a professional distance between yourself and your client. Whilst a healthy business relationship is fine, it is important that you draw a line between your business and home life.

Should you and a client wish to develop a friendship further then you should no longer act for them. Relationships that are too close put you at risk of not doing your job properly for fear of damaging the relationship (such as having to report on the client unfavourably).

If a client wants to spend time with you outside of your working relationship and you feel that this is inappropriate for you to do, you should politely refuse and explain why. If you wish to develop the relationship then that is fine, but you should no longer act for them.

Intimidation threat

Intimidation threats are also often created by the failure of an accountant to maintain sufficient professional distance between themselves and their client. They may occur where an accountant regularly socialises with a client and the client picks up information about the accountant that they may use against them in their working relationship. Such a threat might also be created where professional distance is maintained, but unfavourable information about the accountant is made public through social media such as Facebook or Twitter.

The best safeguards against intimidation threats are to maintain professional distance at all times and not to do anything in your private life that might reflect unfavourably, or be used against you in your business life.

Should a client attempt to intimidate you it is important to take confidential advice on the matter, especially if they threaten to damage your career. In some situations it may be best to report the matter to your manager or senior partner in the practice because if you don't it might come to their attention anyway and it will look like you have tried to hide it from them.

Advocacy threat

Where an accountant has promoted their client in public they are at risk of damaging their objectivity and independence just as much as failing to maintain professional distance. An initial advocacy may have been wholly legitimate, but it could turn out to be the 'thin end of the wedge' as the client expects them to speak for them on more and more matters.

An accountant should be wary about speaking on behalf of their client and should only do so where it is in connection with specific work they have done for them. The best safeguard is to agree with the client, in advance, the matters that they would be happy to speak for them on. Any requests by the client to speak on other matters should be turned down.

For example, an accountant might be legitimately involved in the sale of a client's business to a third party, such as dealing with queries concerning the financial statements, but it would be inappropriate to agree to requests of the client to meet potential buyers and act as a 'salesperson' for the business.

WHISTLE BLOWING

Whistle blowing is the disclosure by an employee of illegal or unethical practices by his or her employer. Theoretically, this ought to be welcomed as in the public interest – but remember: **confidentiality** is also a very strong value in the accountant's code of ethics. This is an important issue, because:

(a) You are in a position to uncover information that you may feel requires disclosure.

(b) You may be the one who is given information by a concerned employee or whistleblower.

Your employer may have set-up **internal whistle blowing procedures** that should be followed if you suspect your employer, colleague or client has committed, or may commit illegal or unethical acts. These may be, for example, reporting the matter in confidence to an ethics committee or senior manager. You should follow any such procedures before you consider reporting the matter externally.

External whistle blowing

Should you decide to report the matter externally then some protection may be available to you under **Public Interest Disclosure Act 1998**. This protection is in the form of '**the right not to be subjected to any detriment by any act, or any deliberate failure to act, by the employer done on the ground that the worker has made a protected disclosure**'.

For this to apply, the disclosure must be made to **specific parties** (such as the employer, legal adviser, Minister of the Crown, or other prescribed persons) and be classed as a '**protected disclosure**'. Protected disclosures include where:

- A criminal offence has been committed, is being committed or is likely to be committed.

- A person has failed, is failing or is likely to fail to comply with any legal obligation to which he is subject.

- A miscarriage of justice has occurred, is occurring or is likely to occur.

- The health or safety of any individual has been, is being or is likely to be endangered.

- The environment has been, is being or is likely to be damaged.

Information tending to show any matter falling within any one of the preceding points has been, is being or is likely to be deliberately concealed.

Reporting such matters is a very serious event and it is important to take advice before making a decision to report your employer under the Act.

Task 5

You work in a large accounting practice. If you begin to suspect that your manager is using his position in your organisation to launder money, who should you report this to?

	✓
NCA	
The police	
Your firm's MLRO (providing they are not your manager)	

CHAPTER OVERVIEW

- Generally speaking, ethical conduct is **legal conduct**.

- When making an ethical decision, it can help to (i) consider the **consequences** and (ii) consider your own **obligations**.

- A **basic test** is to consider whether you want to be on the receiving end of whatever action you are about to take.

- If you are employed by an organisation, any matter of ethical concern should be raised with your **immediate supervisor**. If you are self-employed, you may need to seek **independent advice**.

- As an accountant you are required to be vigilant for instances of **money laundering** – the attempt to conceal the identity of money created as a consequence of illegal activities.

- Particular ethical issues are raised by performing **taxation services**. When you submit a tax return or computations for a client or employer, you are acting as an agent of the taxpayer.

- You have a **duty** to put forward the best position, in favour of your employer or client. You also have a duty towards the tax authorities to provide information in good faith.

- In any **conflict of loyalties**, the requirements of the law and your professional standards take precedence – although you should use your judgement as to whether they will be seriously compromised enough to take action through grievance or ethics procedures.

- If you are asked, instructed or encouraged to take a course of action that is illegal, or unethical by the standards of your profession, you are **entitled and required to refuse**.

- If you suspect that your employers have committed or may commit an illegal or significant unethical act, your first aim is to persuade them to stop or to put the matter right. If they do not, you may have to make a **disclosure** to an appropriate regulator – but you should seek **independent legal advice**.

- Many instances of **inappropriate client behaviour** are actually consequences of an accountant not creating sufficient professional distance between themselves and the client. It is also important for an accountant to conduct themselves appropriately in their personal lives.

- **Whistle blowing** is the disclosure by an employee of illegal or unethical practices by his or her employer.

TEST YOUR LEARNING

Respond to the following by selecting the appropriate option.

Test 1

A self-employed accountant with an ethical dilemma should seek advice from:

	✓
One of the accountant's employees with ethics training.	
The Ethics Advice line of their professional body or a close friend.	
An independent legal expert or the Ethics Advice line of their professional body.	

Test 2

The maximum period of imprisonment for committing the offence of tipping off is:

	✓
5 years	
7 years	
14 years	

Test 3

Which party is responsible for the accuracy of facts, information and computations used by an accountant performing tax work for a client?

	✓
The client	
The accountant	

Test 4

If you are an employed member of a professional body you owe a duty of loyalty to:

	✓
Your profession and HMRC.	
Your employer and your client.	
Your employer, your profession and the public interest.	

Test 5

In a working in practice situation, if a client requests or instructs you to take a course of action that is unethical or illegal, you are entitled and required in the first instance to:

	✓
Terminate the appointment at once.	
Refuse.	
Report your client to the relevant authorities.	

ANSWERS TO CHAPTER TASKS

CHAPTER 1 – The principles of ethical working

1   This is personal to you, so that you begin to think about your own assumptions and beliefs about what kinds of behaviour are 'OK' and 'not OK'. Some of these may be in line with the ethical values of the AAT and accounting profession (such as being honest, telling the truth, being fair and working hard) and some may not be (such as using your work position for the benefit of family members, or offering gifts as a smoother of business relationships and negotiations). In a way, these instances – where your values differ from the professional standards – are more useful information: you know where your 'blind spots' are, and where you may have to modify your assumptions and habits.

2   There is never any single answer to ethical questions. Everyone will have his or her own ideas about 'right' and 'wrong'. All you can do is to look at the facts and come to your own conclusion.

    (a)   The person is clearly breaking the law and this in itself can be considered unethical behaviour. However, some may consider the reason is ethical and that 'the end justifies the means'. You might consider the reason to be unethical since it puts the parent at risk of prosecution, and this may harm the children in the long run.

    (b)   The pilot may be risking the lives of everyone onboard the aircraft to save the life of just one. You could consider this unethical, but the pilot may have many years of experience in dealing with bad weather, so they consider the risk to be low. Pilots will have their own guidelines for dealing with these situations. Ignoring them may constitute unethical behaviour.

    (c)   You may feel the size of the lottery win determines whether the action is ethical or not. Society may expect those with 'small' wins to keep it for themselves, but if they win millions, they should share it. If the winner comes from a wealthy family, the action may be considered perfectly ethical. For a less well-off family, the apparent selfishness may seem completely unethical.

3   The correct answer is:

	✓
True	
False	✓

Straightforwardness and honesty are related to the fundamental principle of integrity.

4   Continuing professional development (CPD) is important to accountancy professionals as it helps them | maintain | competency in their role.

Accountancy professionals attain competence by passing professional exams and gaining relevant experience. It is the maintenance of professional competence that requires continuing awareness and understanding of relevant technical, professional and business developments and is achieved through CPD.

5   The correct answer is:

	✓
If they are asked for during legal proceedings.	✓
When your manager tells you to disclose the information.	
When writing a report for general circulation within your organisation.	

In this case you have a legal duty to disclose the information.

6   The correct answer is:

	✓
Self-interest	
Advocacy	
Intimidation	✓

'Significant pressure' indicates intimidation threat.

7 The correct answer is:

	✓
The Executive Committee	✓
The FRC Board	
The Conduct Committee	

The Executive Committee overseas the day-to-day work of the FRC.

8 Your answer will depend on the nature of your job and the type of organisation that you work for. Good answers would include issues relating to economic (financial) factors, social factors and the environment.

9 The correct answer is:

	✓
Reputational	
Litigation	
Physical	✓

Damage to assets is a loss which results from physical risk.

10 The correct answer is:

	✓
True	
False	✓

Breach of an ethical code does not make an accountant liable under the criminal law.

CHAPTER 2 – Behaving in an ethical manner I

1   The examples you come up with will be relevant to you or your work. However, some examples of common dishonest behaviour include:

- Stealing property
- Using company information for person gain
- Knowingly selling products with defects
- Damage to physical assets – vandalism
- Using pirated software
- Deliberately producing inaccurate or misleading information

2   The correct answer is:

	✓
Self-review	
Intimidation	✓
Familiarity	
Advocacy	

The accountant faces intimidation in the threat of disciplinary action unless they interpret the accounting standard in a particular way.

3   The correct answer is:

	✓
How profitable the relationship will be.	
Whether acceptance would create any threats to compliance with the fundamental principles.	✓
Whether the client's directors meet the firm's moral and ethical standards.	

Whilst the client's profitability and ethical standards may be considered by the firm, they are not required to be considered under professional ethics.

4   The correct answer is:

	✓
True	✓
False	

The situation might arise where the accountant has to act for one of the clients to the detriment of the other.

5   The correct answer is:

	✓
True	
False	✓

Low fees are permitted providing a quality service can be provided at that price. However the statement goes on to make a disparaging remark about the competition which is contrary to the ethical code.

CHAPTER 3 – Behaving in an ethical manner II

1   Whether it is an ethical issue depends on a number of factors, such as:

The value of the hospitality: a sporting event would not normally be regarded as significant – but it would depend on how lavish the package was (or how rare the tickets).

The circumstances: in this case, the fact that the host is bidding for a major contract might suggest an attempt to influence the decision.

In this case, there is probably no ethical issue for you as you are not the one with the authority to make the decision.

However, due to the fact the tickets are likely to be in high demand and have a high value, and the circumstances, it is likely to be an issue for your manager.

2   Section 4 of the Fraud Act 2006 covers fraud by abuse of position.

3   The Information Commissioner's Office (ICO) maintains a public register of data controllers. If any part of a data controller's register becomes inaccurate then they should notify the ICO within 28 days.

4   The correct answer is:

When your client or employer authorises you.	✔
When HMRC requires you to.	✔
When a court requires you to do so.	✔

These are all circumstances where you are permitted to disclose confidential information.

CHAPTER 4 – Taking appropriate action

1   Examples include: health and safety at work; data protection (use of data held by organisations about individuals); equal opportunity and non-discrimination (including avoiding offensive and harassing behaviour towards others on grounds of sex, race and religious beliefs); and company law (eg on retention of documents). Plus – of course – not committing common law offences such as theft, fraud or assault!

2   The maximum penalty for being found guilty of money laundering is | 14 | years in prison.

3   The correct answer is:

	✔
Provide them with a reasonable estimate based on what you achieved last year.	
Tell them that you will save them as much as possible.	
Tell them that you cannot provide such information.	✔

You should not make any statement or promises in this regard, since you are not realistically in a position to do so.

4   The correct answer is:

	✔
Do nothing as admitting errors will damage your professional reputation.	
Correct the error by adjusting this year's tax return to compensate.	
Tell the client to advise HMRC about the error.	✔

Since you acted for the client with regard to the incorrect return, you should advise the client to inform HMRC. If the client refuses to do so then you should make a report to your firm's MLRO, or to NCA (if you are a sole practitioner).

5 The correct answer is:

	✓
NCA	
The Police	
Your firm's MLRO (providing they are not your manager)	✓

The guidelines on what to do about this are set out in law and regulations in the UK. In this case, you have a clear duty to 'blow the whistle' to the appropriate internal authority (the MLRO).

BPP
LEARNING MEDIA

TEST YOUR LEARNING – ANSWERS

CHAPTER 1 – The principles of ethical working

1 The correct answer is:

	✓
True	
False	✓

Group values are very important, eg in families and friendship groups (which is where we get our ideas from), national cultures and organisations (which establish ethical norms and expectations by which we have to operate).

2 The correct answer is:

	✓
Enhance the reputation and standing of accountants.	✓
Limit the number of members that it has.	
Make sure that accountants are able to earn large salaries.	

The accountancy profession needs to maintain standards of conduct and service among its members in order to be able to enhance the reputation and standing of all accountants (so that, for example, they are able to attract and retain clients).

3 The correct answer is:

	✓
Failure to keep up to date on CPD.	
A personal financial interest in the client's affairs.	✓
Being negligent or reckless with the accuracy of the information provided to the client.	

A personal financial interest in the client's affairs will affect objectivity. Failure to keep up to date on CPD is an issue of professional competence, while providing inaccurate information reflects upon professional **integrity**.

4 The correct answer is:

	✓
Say that you will get back to him when you have looked up the answer.	
Give him the contact details of a friend in your firm who knows all about accounting standards.	
Clarify the limits of your expertise with the client.	✓

This is an issue of technical competence and due care. You should clarify the limits of your expertise with the client, and **then** seek information or guidance from the relevant source.

5 The correct answer is:

Apply safeguards to eliminate or reduce the threat to an acceptable level.	3
Evaluate the seriousness of the threat.	2
Discontinue the action or relationship giving rise to the threat.	4
Identify a potential threat to a fundamental ethical principle.	1

6   The correct answer is:

	✓
It is in the public interest that accountants who fail to comply with standards are taken to court.	
It is in the public interest that accountancy services are carried out to professional standards.	✓

It is in the public interest that accountancy services are performed to professional standards, but failure to do so will not result in an accountant being taken to court. Instead the professional body may take action itself against the accountant under its internal rules.

7   The correct answer is:

	✓
The Institute of Chartered Accountants in England and Wales	✓
The Institute of Chartered Accountants of Scotland	✓
Chartered Accountants Ireland	✓
The Chartered Institute of Management Accountants	
The Association of Chartered Certified Accountants	✓
The Chartered Institute of Public Finance and Accountancy	✓
The Association of Accounting Technicians	
The Financial Reporting Council	

8   The correct answer is:

	✓
Economic (financial)	✓
Marketing	
Environmental	✓
Charity	
Social	✓
Political	

The UN Brundtland report identifies economic (financial), social and environment aspects of an accountant's work.

9 The correct answer is:

	✓
Reputational	
Litigation	
Process	
People	✓
Systems	
Legal	
Event	

The definition is that of people risk.

10 The correct answer is:

	✓
True	
False	✓

Accountants are only expected to keep themselves up-to-date in areas of accountancy relevant to their everyday work.

CHAPTER 2 – Behaving in an ethical manner I

1 The correct answer is:

	✔
True	
False	✔

Discovery of a significant error whilst re-evaluating your work gives rise to a self-review threat.

2 The correct answer is:

	✔
Self-interest	✔
Self-review	
Advocacy	
Familiarity	
Intimidation	

A self-interest threat is created as you now have an interest in the transaction.

3 The correct answer is:

	✔
Providing a second opinion.	✔
Accepting a gift from a supplier.	

Providing a second opinion creates a threat to the fundamental principle of professional competence and due care as you may not be aware of all the information you might need to form a second opinion.

4 The Terrorism Act forms part of UK anti-money laundering legislation.

Anti-money láundering legislation in the UK consists of the Terrorism Act 2000, the Proceeds of Crime Act 2002, and the Money Laundering Regulations 2007 (as amended).

CHAPTER 3 – Behaving in an ethical manner II

1   The correct answer is:

	✓
Self-interest	✓
Self-review	
Advocacy	
Familiarity	

Accepting gifts and hospitality from a client can give rise to self-interest and intimidation threats to objectivity.

2   Being bribed ⬚ is ⬚ an offence under the Bribery Act 2010.

The three other offences under this legislation are bribing another person, bribing a foreign public official and failure by a commercial organisation to prevent bribery.

3   The correct answer is:

	✓
True	
False	✓

Clients' monies must be kept separately from monies belonging to the accountant personally and/or to the practice.

4   The correct answer is:

	✓
True	✓
False	

Failure to notify is an offence under the Data Protection Act.

5   The correct answer is:

	✓
True	✓
False	

Your duty means that you must always respect the confidentiality of information of ex-clients and employers.

CHAPTER 4 – Taking appropriate action

1   The correct answer is:

One of the accountant's employees with ethics training.	
The Ethics Advice line of their professional body or a close friend.	
An independent legal expert or the Ethics Advice line of their professional body.	✓

Employees or close friends should not be asked due to confidentiality issues.

2   The correct answer is:

5 years	✓
7 years	
14 years	

The anti-money laundering legislation makes tipping off an offence, the maximum penalty for which is five years imprisonment or an unlimited fine.

3   The correct answer is:

The client	✓
The accountant	

The client is responsible for the accuracy of facts, information and computations used in the tax work done by the accountant.

4 The correct answer is:

	✓
Your profession and HMRC.	
Your employer and your client.	
Your employer, your profession and the public interest.	✓

An accountant has a responsibility to further the legitimate aims of their employer, profession and the public interest.

5 The correct answer is:

	✓
Terminate the appointment at once.	
Refuse.	✓
Report your client to the relevant authorities.	

The request may have been made in ignorance and good faith, so you should attempt to explain the technical, legal and ethical principles that apply.

Question bank

Chapter 1

Task 1.1

You have recently been helping a corporate client prepare for a takeover of another company. The bid has been a success and the directors of your client are delighted to have acquired this other company at what they consider to be a very good price. In order to thank you for your help in this matter, you and your partner have been offered an all expenses paid week in the company villa in Portugal.

Explain whether you should accept or reject this offer.

....

Task 1.2

A client of your company has just moved their business to another firm. Some time ago, they requested your manager to send over the client's books and records. He did not. Each time they called to chase up the request, it seems that your manager 'screened' the call and never responded.

State the fundamental ethical principle threatened by this situation.

....

Task 1.3

You work for a firm of chartered accountants and are required to fill out a time sheet to record each hour worked for each client each day. Last Friday you forgot to prepare the sheet for the week, and you are now doing it on Monday morning. However you are not absolutely sure how long you worked for each client on Thursday and Friday as, due to pressure of work, you did not record it.

State the fundamental ethical principle threatened by this situation.

....

Task 1.4

While at a party at the weekend, you meet a client of yours who is clearly very concerned about some VAT issues. You know enough about VAT to carry out your daily work, but you are not an expert on the areas of imports and exports on which your client is asking your opinion.

State the fundamental ethical principle threatened by this situation.

....

Task 1.5

Explain the purpose of the 'conceptual framework'.

Task 1.6

'As a professional, you should behave with courtesy and consideration towards anyone with whom you come into contact.'

State the fundamental ethical principle defined above.

Task 1.7

You have strong views in support of a client who is being threatened with legal action by a supplier who is alleging late payment of invoices. You have offered to state publicly your views on the matter, in defence of your client.

State the type of threat to objectivity described above.

Task 1.8

State TWO safeguards created by the profession that protect against threats to compliance with the fundamental ethical principles.

Task 1.9

A 'rules based' approach to ethical problem solving has the advantage that, because things are clear-cut and there is no room for misunderstanding, it is easier to know what to do.

State ONE disadvantage of such an approach.

Task 1.10

Which part of the Financial Reporting Council is supported by the Case Management Committee?

Task 1.11

Explain the role of the International Federation of Accountants (IFAC).

Task 1.12

State the THREE members of the CCAB that are sponsoring members of the AAT.

Task 1.13

State the THREE elements to creating an effective ethical programme for a business.

Task 1.14

Monty, an accountant in practice, performs bookkeeping services for both Stumpy Ltd and Grind Ltd. The companies are in dispute about a series of sales that Stumpy Ltd made to Grind Ltd.

Complete the following statement by identifying the TWO ethical principles which are threatened.

'For Monty, this situation threatens the fundamental principles of...'

Task 1.15

Finance professionals have a number of duties in relation to sustainability. These duties can be split into economic (financial), social and environmental aspects.

State ONE example of a duty for each aspect.

Task 1.16

State what is meant by operational risk.

Task 1.17

Event risks may be classified according to their sources in the external environment.

State TWO types of event risk.

....

Task 1.18

Unethical behaviour by an organisation's managers and employees creates a number of risks that an accountant should be aware of.

State THREE types of risk that result from unethical behaviour.

....

Task 1.19

John is a qualified accountant and has been found guilty of professional misconduct by a disciplinary tribunal of his professional body.

State ONE possible penalty that he could face.

expulsion from membership , fine

Task 1.20

State TWO areas of an accountant's knowledge that are considered critical and must be kept up-to-date.

tax legislation

ethical code

Chapter 2

Task 2.1

James, an accountant in practice, has decided to open his own practice, and as a first marketing step he has decided that his fees will be on average 20% lower than those of his competitors.

Explain whether or not the above situation threatens James's compliance with the fundamental principles.

....

Task 2.2

Matt, an accountant in practice, has been working as a manager on work for an important client of his firm. The work is almost at an end and the information produced by Matt will be used by the client's bank to assess whether to increase its lending to the client. The Finance Director of the client has approached Matt and informally discussed the possibility of a high-profile finance position in his department, stating that the role would be his if the information presents the company in a favourable light.

State TWO threats to the fundamental principles of professional ethics identified by this situation.

....

Task 2.3

Ruchita, an accountant in practice, has been offered a referral fee by another accountant to introduce a client to its business.

State TWO of Ruchita's ethical principles that are threatened by this arrangement.

....

Task 2.4

State what procedures an accountant in practice should complete before taking on a new client, in order to comply with Money Laundering Regulations.

....

Task 2.5

State TWO situations where customer due diligence must be carried out, even on existing clients.

....

Task 2.6

What does the acronym NCA stand for?

....

Task 2.7

State TWO pieces of legislation that form part of the anti-money laundering regulations in the UK.

....

Task 2.8

Explain what is meant by customer due diligence procedures on existing clients. *involve existing records op to date*

....

Task 2.9

A client has told you informally that she expects to inherit money from a recently deceased relative. You initially declined to advise her informally on tax matters since you were not sure of your expertise. However, she has now received a considerable sum from the relative's estate, and wants to consult you on the best thing for her to do with the money.

Explain whether you can give her any advice.
no, is inueshnant advice, Im not qualified

Task 2.10

A client is trying to sell her floristry business, and has asked you to prepare financial statements for the business for a potential buyer that she has found. She has asked that you base your fee upon the eventual selling price of the business.

State the fundamental principle that is threatened in this situation.

....

Task 2.11

State the THREE 'reserved areas' that cannot be offered by an accountant without relevant authorisation.

....

Task 2.12

A client may ask an accountant in practice to provide them with a second opinion on the advice they have received from another accountant.

The code of ethics does not prohibit accountants from giving second opinions, however safeguards should be put in place to protect against threats to ethical principles.

State ONE example of a safeguard that could be used when giving a second opinion.

....

Task 2.13

A member of the public has asked you as an accountant to provide them with a second opinion on advice they have received from another firm. However you will not have access to the books and records the other firm used to prepare their advice because they are still holding onto them.

State the fundamental principle you would be in breach of if you were to provide a second opinion without the books and records.

....

Task 2.14

Explain what a 'contingent fee' is.

....

Task 2.15

Individuals may be classified as 'beneficial owners' under money laundering regulations and accountants in practice may be required to obtain certain evidence about them.

Define the term 'beneficial owner'.

....

Task 2.16

The following statement is from marketing material published by Johnny, an accountant working in practice.

'As a member of the AAT, I provide a superior service to those who are members of ICAS.'

Explain whether this statement is in breach of any of the ethical principles relating to marketing.

Task 2.17

State ONE example of a situation that might create a self-interest threat for an accountant in business.

having financial interest

Task 2.18

State ONE example of a situation that might create a familiarity threat for an accountant in business.

Close relationship with someone who benefit from us

Task 2.19

State ONE example of a situation that might create an advocacy threat for an accountant in practice.

Task 2.20

Bob, an accountant working as a partner in a large practice, has a client who runs a newsagent – but he has heard that another of his clients, a bookshop, is planning to open its own outlet in direct competition.

State which threat to fundamental ethical principles is identified by this situation.

Chapter 3

Task 3.1

Professional distance is most closely associated with which ethical principle?

....

Task 3.2

It is important that accountant in business is aware of inducements because accepting them might create self-interest and intimidation threats to objectivity and confidentiality.

State TWO examples of inducements.

gift, hospitality

Task 3.3

An accountant in business has an annual bonus that is related to the company's reported profits that they help to determine.

Which threat to fundamental ethical principles might be caused by this situation?

self interoses t threat (financial interest)

Task 3.4

Jane is an accountant working in practice. During a recent assignment she identified a number of significant threats to her objectivity.

State TWO examples of safeguards Jane could put in place to eliminate the threats or reduce them to an acceptable level.

....

Task 3.5

An accountant in practice will have a contract with each client for the provision of accountancy services.

State the document that sets out the terms of such a contract.

Discus motter with senior manager

Supervisory procedures, make sure my work is done

Task 3.6

Serena has been offered a bottle of wine for her wine connoisseur husband as a Christmas gift by a client, in appreciation of her work.

Should Serena accept the gift because it is for her husband and not her, refuse the gift, because it is never correct to accept gifts from clients, or accept the gift because it is not likely to be perceived as significant enough to affect her objectivity?

Yes accept. IS not significant to effect objectivity

Task 3.7

The husband of Jessica, an accountant in practice, has made a large loan to Laing Ltd, where Jessica is currently working on an engagement.

State the type of threat presented by this situation and explain the correct course of action that should be taken in the circumstances.

Task 3.8

If you are employed in the UK, the acceptance of gifts may be illegal under which piece of legislation?

Bribery Act 2010 610

Task 3.9

It is important to guard against mishandling client monies in order to prevent being found liable for a prison sentence or fine under which pieces of legislation?

Task 3.10

Sarah, an accountant working in a manufacturing company, has been asked to prepare detailed financial information on a new product of which she has very little knowledge. The accountant who normally deals with this product is away on leave for several weeks, and the information is required urgently as part of a report to shareholders. Sarah is very unsure about her ability to complete the work to her usual high standards.

Explain what Sarah should do in this situation.

Task 3.11

Robert, an accountant, holds a number of shares in his employing company.

State the type of threat could this represent to his objectivity when preparing the company's financial statements.

....

Task 3.12

State the FOUR offences introduced into UK law by the Bribery Act 2010.

....

Task 3.13

A new client has asked you to hold a significant amount of money for them but has declined to tell you what the purpose of this money is.

Explain whether or not you should accept this money.

....

Task 3.14

Glen, an accountant, has just started his own tax advisory business. One of his clients, Joanne, has asked him to keep custody of £25,000 in cash for one month, when it will need to be paid to HM Revenue & Customs.

Explain how Glen should deal with this situation.

....

Task 3.15

Gregory is an accountant in practice who acts as account signatory on behalf of a client, Natalie, who is frequently out of the country and non-contactable on long business trips. Last month Greg transferred £7,000 to himself from one of Natalie's many bank accounts.

State the Fraud Act 2006 offence it most likely that Gregory has committed.

....

Task 3.16

Saskia is an accountant in practice, employed by Evans LLP. She has recently completed an assignment at Lawrence Ltd. Lawrence Ltd is no longer a client of Evans LLP, but Saskia has acquired some information about it that would be of interest to another client, DH Ltd.

Explain whether Saskia is permitted to disclose the information about Lawrence Ltd to DH Ltd.

Task 3.17

State the organisation that has legal powers to ensure that organisations comply with the Data Protection Act.

Task 3.18

State an organisation that has statutory powers to demand confidential information from an accountant.

Task 3.19

Jeremy is a data controller. On 2nd April 20X2 he becomes aware that some data has become inaccurate. On 2nd May 20X2 he informs the Information Commissioner's Office (ICO).

Has Jeremy committed a criminal offence?

Task 3.20

State ONE situation where an accountant in practice should NOT hold a client's monies.

Chapter 4

Task 4.1

You are an accountant working in business.

Explain where you should take any ethical concerns if you cannot resolve them with the other person concerned.

....

Task 4.2

Before an accountant in practice performs taxation services for a client, it is important that the accountant and client have agreed their respective responsibilities.

State the name of the document that contains the respective responsibilities of the accountant and client.

....

Task 4.3

Fred, an accountant, is preparing tax computations for his client, Barney Ltd.

State the party that bears ultimate responsibility for the accuracy of the data and computations.

....

Task 4.4

Pat, an accountant in practice, has become aware of a significant error in a tax return from a previous year for one of her clients, Connor Ltd. Pat was not involved in the preparation of the incorrect tax return.

Explain the correct course of action that Pat should take.

....

Task 4.5

Ruby is an accountant in practice who is responsible for Iris's tax computation. Iris is having financial difficulties so Ruby decides to minimise Iris's tax liability by under-declaring income and over-declaring expenses.

Explain whether or not Ruby has committed a criminal offence.

....

Task 4.6

Sam, an accountant, has misgivings over one of his clients, Avalon Ltd. He believes that the client has undeclared income and has asked the owners to supply him with a general assurance, in writing, that all income is being declared. It is now time to prepare Avalon Ltd's tax return.

Explain what Sam should say to the client in connection with the accuracy of the information they provide him.

Task 4.7

Where an accountant's professional rules and standards conflict with explicit directions given to them by their employer, which takes priority?

Task 4.8

Accountants generally have a duty to report money laundering whenever they come across it.

State ONE exception to this rule.

Task 4.9

State TWO actions that an employer cannot require an accountant to do.

Task 4.10

Jimmy, an accountant, has been employed for some years by Laura LLP. He feels that his department manager Nadia poses a threat to his ability to perform his duties with the appropriate degree of professional behaviour, as she keeps asking him to falsify his timesheets so that she can charge higher fees to clients. Jimmy wishes to make a disclosure to senior management at Laura LLP.

Explain the course of action Jimmy should take in these circumstances.

Task 4.11

Helen is a young, out-going newly qualified accountant working in practice. Whilst on assignment she became friends with Jenny, an employee of the company she was seconded to. On a night out, they had a disagreement, Helen became rowdy and was escorted by the police to the local police station to sober up. Jenny took photos of this and has told Helen that she will post them on a social network unless she does what she asks.

Helen's actions created which threat to her fundamental ethical principles?

···

Task 4.12

Savya is an accountant in practice on an engagement at Paint plc. During the course of the engagement he has heard client staff talking about certain funds, which Savya now believes derive from tax evasion.

Explain the correct course of action for Savya to take.

···

Task 4.13

Explain why written records should be kept of discussions and meetings on ethical issues.

···

Task 4.14

Wilma, an accountant, is leaving her employment with Betty Ltd after a disagreement with her manager over his handling of a bad working relationship with a colleague in the sales department. She has made the reasons for her resignation clear to her employer in her exit interview, and she wants to go to the local newspaper about what she sees as Betty Ltd's failure to listen to her concerns.

Explain whether or not Wilma should report her situation to the local paper.

···

Task 4.15

State TWO factors that need to be balanced when considering whether or not to 'blow the whistle'.

···

Task 4.16

Susie, an accountant employed by Luna plc, is facing significant pressure from her manager to give incorrect information to the company's internal auditors.

State the threat to Susie's fundamental principles identified by the situation and which safeguard against it she should take.

▪▪

Task 4.17

You are an accountant in business and have become aware that the retail company you work for has taken on a full time sales person for its new shop, but when checking the payroll records you can find no mention of this new employee, nor any payments to her.

Explain how you should deal with this situation.

▪▪

Task 4.18

Arousha, an accountant, has been asked by her boss to include information in an important report to the Board of Directors that she knows to be inaccurate.

Explain the threat to fundamental principles identified by the situation and what Arousha should do as a first step.

▪▪

Task 4.19

State ONE example of money laundering.

▪▪

Task 4.20

State the offence of 'tipping off'.

▪▪

Answer bank

Answer bank

Chapter 1

Task 1.1

The correct answer is: Reject offer.

This offer of a free holiday should not be accepted due to the principles of professional behaviour and objectivity. The offer looks disreputable and is of significant value. Such a gift, if accepted, could be seen from an observer's point of view as payment in kind for special favours, or may indicate that you may be biased towards that client in future.

Task 1.2

The correct answer is: Professional behaviour.

This is simply unprofessional behaviour by your manager due to him not acting on a client's instructions and screening their calls to avoid them. You may consider reporting the matter to your in-house ethics committee, if there is one.

Task 1.3

The correct answer is: Integrity.

From a personal point of view this is a matter of integrity. Your clients are charged fees on the basis of the hours that you and other members of the firm work for them, so it is important that the recording of these hours is accurate. Therefore you are right to be concerned about not knowing the precise hours, and should ensure that this situation does not happen again.

Task 1.4

The correct answer is: Professional competence and due care.

This raises issues of professional competence and due care. You know that you do not have the knowledge to answer these questions at this time and in this situation. For your own professional safety, you should make the client clearly aware of this and not be prepared to give any opinion, as this may be relied upon by the client despite the circumstances. The most appropriate form of action would be to make an appointment with the client to discuss the matter properly after you have done some research into these specific areas, or refer them to a colleague with experience in this area.

Task 1.5

The correct answer is:

A problem solving procedure that can be used to give you the best chance of complying with ethical principles.

Task 1.6

The correct answer is: Professional behaviour.

'The principle of professional behaviour imposes an obligation on members to comply with relevant laws and regulations and avoid any action that may bring disrepute to the profession.'

Task 1.7

The correct answer is: Advocacy threat.

The risk is that, since you are prepared to promote your opinion, people will have difficulty in believing that you are objective.

Task 1.8

Correct answers include:

Education, training and experience requirements on entry.

Continuing professional development (CPD).

Corporate governance regulations.

Professional standards.

Professional or regulatory monitoring and disciplinary procedures.

External review of financial reports, returns, communications or information produced by members.

Task 1.9

Correct answers include:

Potential for wriggling out of obligations by finding loopholes.

It promotes a 'tick box' mentality with concern for the letter, rather than the spirit, of the law.

It must legislate for every possible circumstance, resulting in a large number of detailed requirements.

New requirements must be developed as circumstances change.

There is a higher risk of getting swamped by the details and missing the bigger picture.

Tasks 1.10

The correct answer is: The Conduct Committee.

This body is supported by the Case Management Committee.

Tasks 1.11

'IFAC is an international body representing all the major accountancy bodies across the world. Its mission is to develop the high standards of professional accountants and enhance the quality of services they provide.'

Task 1.12

The correct answer is: ICAEW, ICAS and CIPFA.

These are the AAT's sponsoring members.

Task 1.13

The correct answer is:

Active leadership, buy-in and training.

Task 1.14

The correct answer is:

For Monty, this situation threatens the fundamental principles of objectivity and confidentiality.

Task 1.15

There is more than one possible correct answer to this question. Credit will be given for any relevant answer.

Correct answers might include:

Economic (financial) aspects

Supporting clients or their organisation to be profitable, supporting other local businesses, paying suppliers on time, looking for ways to improve organisational efficiency.

Social aspects

Supporting corporate governance policies, consulting the local community when making decisions on investing or relocating resources.

Environmental aspects

Supporting policies to manage resources and running the organisation in a sustainable way, not printing emails unless necessary, turning lights off at the end of the day, recycling office materials.

Task 1.16

The correct answer is:

Operational risk is the risk of loss arising from the day-to-day business of the company through its processes, staff, systems or external events.

Task 1.17

The correct answer is any two from the following:

Physical risk, social risk, political risk, economic risk.

Task 1.18

The correct answer is any three from the following:

Damage to the company's brand or image.

Reduced levels of employee performance and corporate productivity.

Increased absenteeism.

Reduced employee discipline and increased conflict between individuals within the organisation.

Increased employee turnover rates.

Increased dysfunctional behaviour.

Reduced corporate value.

Task 1.19

The correct answer is any one from the following:

A fine.

Expulsion from membership of the professional body.

Task 1.20

The correct answer is any two from the following:

Reporting and auditing standards.

Ethical codes.

Tax and company legislation.

Criminal law affecting accountants.

Other regulations affecting accounting, reporting, tax compliance, audit and the accounting and finance profession.

Chapter 2

Task 2.1

The correct answer is:

There is no threat providing James can give a quality service for that price. If fees are mentioned in promotional material, James must ensure that the statements are not misleading, eg about what is covered and how the fees are calculated, to comply with the fundamental principles of integrity and professional behaviour.

Task 2.2

The correct answer is: Self-interest and intimidation.

The self-interest threat comes from the high-profile role on offer if the information is presented favourably. The intimidation threat is implied from the situation – if it is not favourable he will not get the role.

Task 2.3

The correct answers are:

- Objectivity
- Professional competence and due care

Task 2.4

The correct answer is: Customer due diligence procedures.

Customer due diligence must be performed on all new clients before acting for them.

Task 2.5

The correct answer is any two from the following:

The member enters a professional relationship with the client.

The member acts for the client in a transaction over £15,000 or the sterling equivalent.

There is a suspicion of money laundering or terrorist financing.

There are doubts over previously obtained customer identification.

At an appropriate time on a risk sensitive basis.

Task 2.6

The correct answer is: National Crime Agency

Task 2.7

The correct answer is: Any two from the following:

The Proceeds of Crime Act 2002, The Terrorism Act 2000 and The Money Laundering Regulations 2007.

Task 2.8

The correct answer is:

Customer due diligence procedures on existing clients involve keeping existing records up to date and undertaking appropriate customer due diligence procedures on any transactions that seem inconsistent with existing knowledge of the client's business or risk profile.

Task 2.9

The correct answer is:

The situation presents what is effectively a request for investment advice, and you are not qualified to give it.

Task 2.10

The correct answer is: Objectivity.

Fees that depend on the outcome of an assignment are known as contingency fees and they must not be charged for financial reporting services as they are a threat to objectivity.

Task 2.11

The correct answer is: Insolvency work, audit and investment business.

These are the three 'reserved areas'.

Task 2.12

There is more than one possible correct answer to this question. Credit will be given for any relevant answer.

Correct answers might include:

Seeking permission to contact the other accountant.

If permission for contacting the other accountant is refused, to reconsider whether it is appropriate to give the opinion.

Making the client aware of any limitations surrounding the opinion.

Providing the other accountant with a copy of the second opinion.

Task 2.13

The correct answer is: Professional competence and due care.

Professional competence is at risk if you do not base your opinion on the same set of facts as the other accountant or if you have insufficient evidence to make a decision.

Task 2.14

The correct answer is:

A contingent fee is a fee that is on a predetermined basis (such as a percentage) which relates to the outcome of work done or a transaction.

Task 2.15

The correct answer is:

A 'beneficial owner' is an individual who owns 25% or more of the client or the transaction property.

Task 2.16

The correct answer is:

The statement does not comply with the ethical principles relating to marketing because it makes disparaging and unsubstantiated comparisons to the work of others.

Task 2.17

There is more than one possible correct answer to this question. Credit will be given for any relevant answer.

Examples of situations that might create a self-interest threat to members in business include:

Having a financial interest (such as shares or loans) in the employer.

Receiving financial incentives and rewards based on the organisation's profit.

Opportunities to use corporate assets for own use.

Where there is a risk of losing a job or promotion.

Commercial pressure from external organisations.

Task 2.18

There is more than one possible correct answer to this question. Credit will be given for any relevant answer.

Examples of situations that might create a familiarity threat to members in business include:

Having a close or personal relationship with someone who might benefit from your influence.

Having a long-standing business association with a contact who might influence your decisions.

Accepting a gift or preferential treatment which might be thought to influence your decision.

Task 2.19

There is more than one possible correct answer to this question. Credit will be given for any relevant answer.

Examples of situations that might create an advocacy threat to members in practice include:

Where the member promotes shares in a client company that is listed on the stock market.

Acting on behalf of a client which is in litigation or dispute with a third party.

Task 2.20

The correct answer is:

There is a conflict of interest because Bob has to act for two competing businesses.

Chapter 3

Task 3.1

The correct answer is:

Professional distance is closely associated with the ethical principle of objectivity.

....

Task 3.2

There is more than one possible correct answer to this question. Credit will be given for any relevant answer.

Examples of inducements might include:

Gifts, hospitality, preferential treatment and appeals to friendship and loyalty.

....

Task 3.3

The correct answer is:

An accountant that has a financial interest in their employer might face a self-interest threat.

....

Task 3.4

There is more than one possible correct answer to this question. Credit will be given for any relevant answer.

Examples of safeguards might include:

Withdrawing from the assignment team

Put supervisory procedures in place to ensure her work is reviewed

Discuss the matter with senior management in the firm

....

Task 3.5

The correct answer is:

The engagement letter sets out the terms of the contract between accountant and client.

Task 3.6

The correct answer is: Accept the gift because it is not likely to be perceived as significant enough to affect her objectivity.

Task 3.7

The correct answer is:

The situation presents a self-interest threat.

The correct course of action is to remove Jessica from the engagement.

Task 3.8

The correct answer is:

If you are employed in the UK, the acceptance of gifts may be illegal under the Bribery Act 2010.

Task 3.9

The correct answer is:

It is important to guard against mishandling client monies in order to prevent being found liable for a prison sentence or fine under the Fraud Act, Theft Act or Proceeds of Crime Act.

Task 3.10

The correct answer is:

Sarah should let her manager know that the task is outside the boundaries of her expertise and experience.

It is important to be realistic and responsible and let people know when you are not confident about completing a task, especially when it is a significant one.

....

Task 3.11

The correct answer is: Self-interest.

If such threats are significant safeguards will have to be put in place.

....

Task 3.12

The correct answer is: Bribing another person, being bribed, bribing a foreign public official, failure by a commercial organisation to prevent bribery.

....

Task 3.13

The correct answer is: You should not accept the money because you do not know the purpose of the funds. Accountants cannot hold clients' monies without verifying the commercial purpose of the transaction.

....

Task 3.14

The correct answer is: Glen should hold the money, but keep it separate from his business' funds.

Clients' monies should be kept separately from monies belonging to the member personally and/or to the practice.

....

Task 3.15

The correct answer is: Gregory is most likely to have committed fraud by abuse of position.

....

Task 3.16

The correct answer is: Saskia is not permitted to disclose the information about Lawrence Ltd. The principle of confidentiality applies even after the assignment, or the contractual relationship with the client is over.

Task 3.17

The correct answer is: The Information Commissioner's Office (ICO).

Task 3.18

The correct answer is: HM Revenue & Customs (HMRC).

There are other equally valid answers – such as the police, security services and SOCA.

Task 3.19

The correct answer is: Yes. The ICO must be informed within 28 days of any entry becoming inaccurate or out of date – failure to do so is a criminal offence.

Task 3.20

The correct answer is any one from the following.

Where the monies are in relation to investment business and the member is not regulated.

Where there is reason to believe the funds are 'criminal property'.

Where there is no justification for holding the monies (eg they are not related to a service the member provides).

Where the member has a condition on their licence that prohibits them from dealing with client monies.

Chapter 4

Task 4.1

The correct answer is: You should take ethical concerns to your immediate supervisor or as directed by an ethical reporting procedure.

....

Task 4.2

The correct answer is: The letter of engagement.

....

Task 4.3

The correct answer is: Barney Ltd (the client) is ultimately responsible for the accuracy of the data and computations.

....

Task 4.4

The correct answer is: Pat should immediately advise Connor Ltd and recommend that they inform HM Revenue & Customs.

....

Task 4.5

The correct answer is: Yes – Ruby has committed an offence under the Proceeds of Crime Act.

For the purposes of money laundering, the proceeds of deliberate tax evasion are just as much 'criminal property' as money from drug trafficking or theft.

....

Task 4.6

The correct answer is: Sam should say to the client that they bear ultimate responsibility for the accuracy of the facts, information and tax computations, and that he can refuse to be associated with their tax return if he suspects that it is incomplete or inaccurate.

....

Task 4.7

The correct answer is: The rules and standards of the profession take priority where they clash with those of an accountant's employer.

Task 4.8

The correct answer is: Any one from the following.

When knowledge or suspicion of the offence was not obtained in the accountant's normal course of business (for example at a social event).

When knowledge or suspicion of the offence was obtained in privileged circumstances.

If there is a reasonable excuse not to report it.

Task 4.9

There is more than one possible correct answer to this question. Credit will be given for any relevant answer.

Correct answers might include:

Break the law, break rules and standards of the accounting profession, significantly misrepresent facts, lie or mislead regulators or auditors, facilitate or be part of the handling of unethical or illegal earnings.

Task 4.10

The correct answer is: Jimmy should follow any internal procedures in place for employees such as him to report unethical behaviour.

Task 4.11

The correct answer is:

Helen's actions have resulted in an intimidation threat.

Task 4.12

The correct answer is: Savya must report his suspicions so as to avoid a charge under POCA of failure to report. The proceeds of tax evasion are criminal property and it is therefore money laundering.

Task 4.13

The correct answer is: Written records should be kept to ensure that there is evidence of any advice received.

This will help to protect you in any legal proceedings that may result; if your subsequent conduct is prosecuted, for example – or if you are unfairly victimised or dismissed for taking a stand on the issue.

Task 4.14

The correct answer is: Wilma is bound by a duty of confidentiality not to talk about her reasons for leaving, and there does not appear to be any legal duty to disclose what has happened. Therefore she should not report her situation to the local paper.

Task 4.15

The correct answer is: Confidentiality and public interest.

Whistle-blowing is the disclosure by an employee of illegal or unethical practices by his or her employer. This can be in the public interest – but confidentiality is also a very strong value to consider.

Task 4.16

The correct answer is: Susie's situation represents an intimidation threat to her fundamental principles and she should implement the safeguard of obtaining advice, for instance from her professional body.

Task 4.17

The correct answer is: The first step is probably to speak to your manager about your concerns, and it may then be suggested that you speak to the payroll department in general terms about the importance of accurate reporting. In this situation you will probably be suspicious that the employee is being paid in cash in order to avoid the tax consequences of employment. Payroll fraud is an offence that is reportable to SOCA.

Task 4.18

The correct answer is: This is an intimidation threat, and as a first step Arousha should refuse to be associated with incorrect information. If her manager persists in his request, Arousha may need to take legal advice.

Task 4.19

There is more than one possible correct answer to this question. Credit will be given for any relevant answer.

A correct answer might be: Receiving benefits obtained through bribery.

There are many activities that constitute money laundering, other examples must be connected to acquiring, using, controlling, concealing, disguising, converting, transferring or removing criminal property. Criminal property is any benefit obtained through criminal activity.

Task 4.20

The correct answer is: Tipping off involves disclosing something that might prejudice an investigation.

AAT AQ2013 SAMPLE ASSESSMENT
PROFESSIONAL ETHICS

Time allowed: 2 hours 30 minutes

AAT AQ2013 SAMPLE ASSESSMENT

Instructions to candidates

To 'state' something, you need to answer with a fact. If you are asked to 'explain' something you need to state the relevant fact and then give brief reason(s) for why the fact is the right answer. If you are asked to 'describe' you should set out what is involved without further explanation.

Task 1 (8 marks)

(a) **Which body is responsible for regulating the UK accountancy profession as a whole?**

(b) **Which body sets global ethical standards for accountants?**

(c) **State TWO of the four sponsoring bodies of AAT.**

(1)

(2)

(d) **State TWO of the three statutory regulated (reserved) areas in accountancy and finance.**

(1)

(2)

(e) **All professional accountants have five ethical principles which they have a duty to comply with. Explain whether this duty is more important for professional accountants in practice rather than those in business.**

Task 2 (12 marks)

(a) **Professional accountants are required to undertake continuing professional development (CPD). State which ONE of the five fundamental principles is safeguarded by CPD.**

(b) Charis is a professional accountant with her own small practice. She prepares sets of accounts and tax returns for a wide range of sole traders.

In light of her client base, explain ONE area of technical knowledge in which Charis must keep up-to-date.

(c) **Complete the following statement:**

A professional accountant who complies with the law, brings no disrepute on the profession and is perceived as being ethical by other people has complied with the fundamental principle of...

(d) Frank, a professional accountant in practice, has acted outside the limits of his professional expertise in working for his client Nancy. Nancy has incurred a regulatory fine as a result.

State TWO grounds on which Nancy may be able to seek compensation from Frank for this loss.

(1)

(2)

(e) Christie is a professional accountant in practice who has had Alpha Ltd as a client for many years. In her professional capacity, Christie has been asked by Alpha Ltd's new landlord to give a written reference confirming that the company is likely to be able to pay rent over the next five years. Alpha Ltd is paying Christie a large fee for supplying the reference.

(i) **Is it acceptable practice for Christie to include a disclaimer of liability in the written reference?**

(Choose an option – Yes/No)

(ii) **If Christie gives the reference, even though she knows that Alpha Ltd has no means of paying the rent, what kind of fraud is she committing?**

(f) Marion, a professional accountant in practice, gives Larch Ltd an opinion on the application of accounting principles to the company's specific transactions. Marion knew that she was forming her opinion on the basis of inadequate information.

In addition to integrity, state which other ONE of Marion's fundamental ethical principles is threatened by this situation. Explain the reasons for your answer.

(g) Henry is a professional accountant. He finished his exams and qualified a year ago.

State ONE way in which Henry can ensure he keeps up-to-date with technical changes in accounting and reporting.

Task 3 (5 marks)

Leonardo is a professional accountant in practice as a sole practitioner. His client, Alana, has given Leonardo £10,000 to hold on her behalf so that he can transfer money for her to HM Revenue & Customs (HMRC) when necessary. Leonardo now has good reason to believe the money is criminal property.

(a) **With what crime could Leonardo be charged if he retains Alana's money without notifying the authorities?**

(b) Leonardo has taken custody of monies for another client so that he can carry out the client's instructions.

    (i) **In what legal capacity does Leonardo hold these client monies for the client?**

    (ii) **For what TWO crimes could Leonardo be prosecuted if he fails to properly account to the client for the monies?**

        (1)
        (2)

    (iii) **May Leonardo retain these monies in his practice bank account?**

Task 4 (5 marks)

(a) Professional accountants must maintain the confidentiality of information which is obtained in circumstances that give rise to a duty of confidentiality.

Is this an ethical principle only, a legal obligation only, or both an ethical principle and a legal obligation?

(Choose an option)

(b) **Explain whether a professional accountant is allowed to use knowledge, information and experience gained from a previous employer in a new job.**

(c) George is a professional accountant in practice. He has several pieces of confidential information about his client Mabel.

State whether it may be appropriate for George to disclose the information in the following circumstances:

    (i) **Disclosure to the appropriate public authority of Mabel's infringement of the criminal law.**

    (ii) **Disclosure which is not required by law but which is authorised by Mabel.**

Tasks 5 – 9

Tasks 5 – 9 are based on the following project scenario and the six matters listed. Each task indicates which of the six specific matters is/are relevant to the task.

Project scenario

ABC Co is a well-established firm of accountants with a single office in the city of Standley. In total ABC Co employs ten fully qualified professional accountants, three part-qualified student accountants and six administrative staff.

Any letters received in the post by ABC Co are opened immediately by one of the administrative staff. They are then left in a closed folder on the relevant person's desk.

ABC Co's clients include:

- Straithard Ltd, a trading company run by Mick Gurdy.

- Williams Ltd, a small painting and decorating company with annual revenue of £50,000 and annual profits of £10,000.

- Crawthorne Ltd, a company which manufactures high quality wooden furniture to order.

- Unwin Ltd and Idris Ltd, both of which are technology companies based in Standley.

- Bradley Ltd, a new client operating in the transport sector.

You are Chris, one of the three part-qualified student accountants at ABC Co. You report to Ian, one of the fully qualified professional accountants.

Recently the following six matters have come to light.

Matter 1

Eliza Brown, one of the fully qualified professional accountants in ABC Co, has been off sick for a week. Your line manager Ian asked you to go through the mail folder on Eliza's desk to see if there was anything that needed to be dealt with urgently. You found the following note:

Note from: Mick Gurdy, Straithard Ltd

Addressed to: Eliza Brown, ABC Co

Eliza

I'm pretty disappointed that you haven't answered my emails or texts. I thought I had made it clear to you that I'll let you have that £500 you need for your holiday but only if you go ahead and include on the company's tax return the revenue figure that I gave you. I don't care that it's much less than the figure from the accounts. You know that if you don't do as I say by the end of the month I'm going to tell your firm about the other ways in which you have helped me manipulate our figures in the past. This is your last chance.

Mick

Matter 2

Williams Ltd, a small painting and decorating company, has unexpectedly requested ABC Co help it to apply for a gambling licence and to look for premises for a casino costing £10 million.

Matter 3

In response to best-practice guidelines issued by its trade organisation and encouragement from ABC Co, Crawthorne Ltd has drafted a six-point Code of Practice for use within the company's finance function. You have been handed the following extract:

Confidential

Extract from draft Code of Practice for finance function of Crawthorne Ltd

For reference only by Crawthorne Ltd's finance function staff in the course of their duties

Drafted by: Kenny Long, Assistant Accountant, Crawthorne Ltd

Each member of Crawthorne Ltd's finance function staff will ensure that:

(1) Any request for information from regulators, staff, customers or suppliers will be treated in a timely manner and with openness, honesty, accuracy *(want info?)* and respect.

(2) Personal information held in the finance function will be treated with respect and in line with relevant statutory requirements. *conf*

(3) Purchase prices paid to suppliers for goods and services will be reviewed by a senior person in terms of their fairness to both parties if a complaint is raised by the supplier.

(4) Payments to all suppliers will be made so that funds are received by them no later than 30 days after the relevant invoice has been recorded, unless some other arrangement has been expressly agreed with the supplier.

> (5)   No individual finance function member will accept an offer of a gift or hospitality from any person unless (a) its worth is less that £20 AND (b) the same offer is made to all or substantially all of the person's business associates.
>
> (6)   Any complaint from Crawthorne Ltd employees about the amount or timing of a payroll payment will be reviewed and responded to within 24 hours of its receipt in the finance function.

When looking at the company's file you also note that Crawthorne Ltd recently asked ABC Co for advice in relation to an e-mail received from one of its customers, Tolly Ltd. Tolly Ltd had ordered furniture to a value of £200 from Crawthorne Ltd.

> From: r.askew@tollyltd.com
> To: k.long@crawthorneltd.co.uk
> Subject: Payment error
>
> Hi Kenny
>
> Stupidly we have made a transfer of funds to you in error, even though you have not yet delivered the furniture to us. Our transfer is for £20,000. It would be embarrassing to have the money repaid to our bank account so could you transfer £19,800 instead to the bank account of: Japes Ltd, sort code 30-25-94, account number 98924983? You can keep hold of £200 in advance payment of your invoice to us once raised.
>
> Ryan Askew, Tolly Ltd

You note that on the advice of ABC Co, Crawthorne Ltd did not make the requested transfer because of the possibility of this action implicating Crawthorne Ltd in illegal activity by Tolly Ltd. The matter is still being investigated.

Matter 4

For several years Bernard, one of ABC Co's fully qualified professional accountants, has dealt with two competing technology companies, Unwin Ltd and Idris Ltd. The two companies have existing premises in Standley Science Park, where a new building has just been completed. Idris Ltd and Unwin Ltd are both putting in a bid to lease the whole of the new building. They each asked Bernard to act for them in relation to the bid. When the companies realised they were both interested in leasing the same building, Idris Ltd offered Bernard an extra £3,000 to act for it exclusively; Unwin Ltd also offered Bernard an additional £3,000 for exclusive representation. Neither company is willing for Bernard to act for both parties with respect to the lease.

Matter 5

Very recently ABC Co started an engagement for a new client operating in the transport sector, Bradley Ltd, following appropriate customer due diligence procedures. Sam, one of ABC Co's fully qualified professional accountants, had been working on Bradley Ltd's accounts for a short time when she realised that a serious tax error had been made in the previous period's tax return. The tax error was made by Bradley Ltd's financial controller, Vince, and led to a large underpayment of tax. Sam has brought this error to Vince's attention but the directors of Bradley Ltd categorically refuse to disclose the error to HMRC. Sam needs to decide firstly whether ABC Co should continue to act for Bradley Ltd and secondly whether she has any external reporting requirements in respect of Bradley Ltd.

Matter 6

One of ABC Co's newest fully qualified professional accountants, Jamie, is very keen to promote sustainability and sustainable development in the firm, and has made a presentation to the firm's staff which mentions:

- The Brundtland definition of sustainability.

- That professional accountants are obliged to support sustainability as far as they are able in the context of their work.

- That ABC Co should champion sustainability by encouraging its clients to focus on their 'triple bottom line'.

Unfortunately no-one is clear about what Jamie actually meant.

Task 5 (10 marks)

Refer to the Project Scenario and Matter 1.

(a) **Explain which THREE of Eliza Brown's fundamental principles are most threatened by the situation outlined in Mick Gurdy's note.**

(b) **In terms of the conceptual framework, explain the TWO threats being faced by Eliza.**

integrity = including false figures

objectivity = accepting gifts may compromise you professional judgment

problem beh = submitting false figures, breach of law

Task 6 (10 marks)

Refer to the Project Scenario and Matters 2 and 3.

(a) Explain whether ABC Co should conduct customer due diligence (CDD) procedures with respect to Williams Ltd's request about the gambling licence and casino.

(b) Explain THREE of Crawthorne Ltd's key ethical organisational values with reference to its draft Code of Practice.

(c) Explain whether Crawthorne Ltd's Code of Practice will be a statutory code once it is implemented.

(d) Draft a seventh point for Crawthorne Ltd's draft Code of Practice to address the type of situation that the company is facing in relation to Tolly Ltd.

Task 7 (10 marks)

Refer to the Project Scenario and Matter 4.

(a) Explain which TWO of Bernard's fundamental principles are threatened by the fact that both Idris Ltd and Unwin Ltd are bidding for the lease on the same building in Standley Science Park.

(b) Describe the ethical conflict resolution process that Bernard should undertake in deciding how to act in respect of this matter. Assume that he will be able to resolve the conflict of interest without external professional advice.

(c) Assuming he decides he can act for one of the clients, explain TWO issues Bernard must consider when carrying out the engagement.

Task 8 (10 marks)

Refer to the Project Scenario and Matter 5.

(a) (i) Explain the actions Sam must take in respect of Bradley Ltd.

  (ii) Explain the consequences for Sam if the actions in (a) (i) are NOT taken.

(b) Explain what actions Vince should take about Bradley Ltd's refusal to report to HMRC, and what protection these actions will give him.

Task 9 (10 marks)

Refer to the Project Scenario and Matter 6.

(a) **Explain the TWO key aspects of sustainability as set out in the UN Brundtland Report.**

(b) **Explain the nature of the professional accountant's obligation to uphold the values of sustainability.**

(c) **Explain what Jamie meant by 'the triple bottom line' for ABC Co's clients.**

(d) **Describe for your accountant colleagues in ABC Co FOUR ways in which they can seek to support sustainability and sustainable development within ABC Co itself.**

••

AAT AQ2013 SAMPLE ASSESSMENT
PROFESSIONAL ETHICS

ANSWERS

Task 1

(a) The Financial Reporting Council (FRC).

(b) International Ethics Standards Board for Accountants (IESBA) or International Federation of Accountants (IFAC).

(c) Any two of the following: ICAEW, CIMA, CIPFA or ICAS.

(d) Any two of the following: Audit, investment business or insolvency.

(e) It is EQUALLY important for accountants in business to comply as for those in practice, because these are the fundamental principles of the profession even if how they are complied with is different.

Task 2

(a) Professional competence and due care.

(b) Identify one of: regulation of accounting; tax legislation/compliance; money laundering regulation; accounting/reporting standards.

Reason given for importance of area selected for sole traders because clients are businesses which must comply with requirement for accurate accounts preparation and tax returns/Charis needs to protect herself re money laundering.

(c) Professional behaviour.

(d) An action for breach of contract. An action for professional negligence.

(e) (i) Yes
(ii) Fraud by false representation

(f) Professional competence and due care. Marion is not acting diligently nor is she in accordance with applicable professional standards by giving an opinion without having access to adequate information.

(g) Read professional journals; attend technical update courses; comply with CPD requirements.

Task 3

(a) Money laundering.

(b) (i)   In trust/as a trustee
     (ii) Theft, fraud by abuse of position
     (iii) No

Task 4

(a) BOTH an ethical principle and a legal obligation.

(b) An accountant is allowed to use general knowledge and experience from a previous employer but NOT specific information from that employer that is covered by the duty of confidentiality.

(c) (i)   Yes, may be appropriate to disclose.
     (ii) Yes, may be appropriate to disclose.

Task 5

(a) The THREE fundamental principles most threatened are:

- Integrity: including false figures is being associated with misleading information, and it is dishonest.

- Objectivity: giving in to threats/pressure/the offer of payment is allowing a conflict of interest/undue influence to override or compromise professional judgement.

- Professional behaviour: submitting false figures to HMRC is in breach of relevant laws and regulations and brings the accounting profession into disrepute.

(b)
- Self-interest threat from Mick's offer of £500 for her holiday.

- Intimidation threat from Mick's statement that he will report her past behaviour to her firm.

Task 6

(a) Yes, ABC Co should conduct CDD as these suggested transactions appear to be inconsistent with prior knowledge of the client and the client's normal business which is painting and decorating on a small scale.

(b) Three from the following:

- Reporting financial and regulatory information clearly and on time (refer to point 1).

- Being transparent with colleagues, customers and suppliers (refer to point 1).

- Being open and honest by identifying when it is appropriate to accept gifts and hospitality (refer to point 5).

- Paying suppliers a fair price and on time (refer to points 3 and 4).

- Providing fair treatment to employees (refer to points 2 and 6).

(c) No, it will not be statutory. The code has been created in response only to the trade organisation's best practice guidelines and ABC Co's encouragement, so it is clearly a voluntary one prepared by Crawthorne Ltd for its own use/The code cannot be statutory since that would be created under legislation/regulation/case law and used by many companies.

(d) 'Point 7: Finance function staff will remain vigilant to the risks of being unwittingly involved in money laundering, bribery and other illegal acts. In particular, any overpayment by a customer will be thoroughly investigated by a senior member of finance function staff and only repaid to the customer once it has been established that it is right/legal to do so.'

Task 7

(a) Objectivity – because it is difficult to act without a perception of bias when the two clients' interests are in such conflict because they both want the lease; and Confidentiality – because he has confidential information in respect of each client.

(b) Bernard should:

- Consider relevant facts/ethical issues involved/his fundamental principles/any established procedures in ABC Co

- Establish alternative courses of action, establish which is most consistent with the fundamental principles and establish the consequences of each

- Seek advice about the matter within ABC Co, and document the substance of the issue and discussions

(c) In acting for one of the clients Bernard should consider instituting appropriate safeguards so that his familiarity with the other client does not affect his professional judgement/objectivity, and so that he does not breach confidentiality re the other party.

· ·

Task 8

(a) (i) Sam must inform Bradley Ltd that she/ABC Co can no longer act for Bradley Ltd because funds dishonestly retained after discovery of a tax error become criminal property so their retention amounts to money laundering by Bradley Ltd. Sam must make an internal report on the matter to ABC Co's MLRO.

(ii) If Sam further facilitates Bradley Ltd's retention of the funds related to the tax error by continuing to act for it, Sam will herself be engaged in money laundering. As ABC Co is a firm in the regulated sector, if the action required under the Proceeds of Crime Act is not taken then Sam will have committed the crime of failure to disclose.

(b) As he is now aware of the error, Vince should report to SOCA that he suspects Bradley Ltd of money laundering because it has refused to notify the matter to HMRC. He will be protected from a claim for breach of confidentiality when making this report. Knowing he may have been involved in money laundering, Vince needs to make an authorised disclosure to SOCA which may help protect him from a charge that he himself, in making the error, was engaged in money laundering.

· ·

Task 9

(a) 'Meeting the needs of the present without compromising the ability of future generations to meet their own needs'.

(b) Obligation is part of professional accountant's responsibility to act in the public interest. This includes supporting sustainability and sustainable development and considering the risks to society as a whole of not acting sustainably.

(c) Taking social, environmental and economic (financial) factors into account when measuring position and performance for clients or when assisting with their decision-making.

(d) Any four from the following:

- Promote sustainable practices through ABC Co re services, clients, fellow employees, the workplace, the supply chain and business functions/processes.

- Encourage long-term responsible management/use of resources within ABC Co.

- Facilitate ABC Co being run in a sustainable manner.

- Highlight within ABC Co the risks of not acting sustainably.

- Take social/environmental/ethical factors into account when assisting with decision-making or performance/position measurement.

BPP PRACTICE ASSESSMENT
PROFESSIONAL ETHICS

Time allowed: 2 hours 30 minutes

PRACTICE ASSESSMENT

PETH BPP practice assessment

Instructions to candidates

To 'state' something, you need to answer with a fact. If you are asked to 'explain' something you need to state the relevant fact and then give brief reason(s) for why that fact is the right answer. If you are asked to 'describe' you should set out what is involved without further explanation.

The time allowed to complete this Professional Ethics in Accounting and Finance assessment is **2 hours and 30 minutes**.

Task 1 (8 marks)

(a) Which international organisation, of which the AAT is a member, is responsible for ethics in the accounting profession worldwide?

(b) To which UK organisation should suspicions of money laundering activity be reported?

(c) State TWO types of lawsuit that would be heard in a civil court.

(1)

(2)

(d) State TWO of the three committees of the Financial Reporting Council (FRC) that report directly into the FRC board.

(1)

(2)

(e) Business organisations often introduce codes of conduct to regulate the behaviour of employees. Explain the benefit of codes of conduct to the organisations that introduce them.

Task 2 (12 marks)

(a) State FOUR types of legal action that an accountant who fails to act with sufficient expertise might face.

(b) Describe the level of skill that an accountant is expected to demonstrate in their work.

(c) State the legal remedy that is available to a party who suffers losses as a consequence of their accountant's professional negligence.

(d) Complete the following statement:

An accountant who has acted diligently in accordance with applicable technical and professional standards when providing professional services has complied with the fundamental principle of...

(e) Janet, an accountant, has been told that the future of her job depends upon the success of her company's latest product, which she knows has faults but which is being promoted widely with no mention of them. She is being asked to sell the product to her friends.

State the type of threat to her professional integrity that Janet faces.

(f) Vanessa, an accountant, has been asked to provide a reference to a third party about one of her clients.

State ONE way that Vanessa can minimise the risk of being sued for damages by the third party.

(g) Faye is an accountant in practice and would like to expand the types of work that she offers her clients, however she understands that certain work in 'reserved areas' cannot be carried out unless she is supervised in doing so.

State TWO of the 'reserved areas' of work.

(1)

(2)

••

Task 3 (5 marks)

(a) Otto is an accountant in practice who looks after the tax affairs of a number of clients. The practice frequently makes payments to, and receives payments from HMRC on behalf of clients.

Explain THREE safeguards that Otto should put in place when handling clients' monies.

(b) Samantha is a junior member of staff at Otto's practice. One client, who is under investigation by the police for fraud, has asked her if she could hold £10,000 for him in a client account.

Explain whether Samantha should agree to the client's request.

••

Task 4 (5 marks)

(a) **State THREE circumstances where a professional accountant is permitted to disclose confidential information.**

(b) Lana is an accountant in business and is the manager of a busy finance department. Recently she has been involved in deciding which supplier should be awarded a contract to provide the company with Material X.

Last week she discovered that Brian, a member of her team, was paid by Company Y, a prospective supplier of Material X, to supply it with the details of its competitors' quotes.

Explain whether Lana is in breach of the fundamental principle of confidentiality.

••

Tasks 5 – 9

Tasks 5 – 9 are based on the following project scenario and the five matters listed. Each task indicates which of the five specific matters is/are relevant to the task.

Project scenario

XYZ is a medium-sized accountancy practice with a range of clients, from small sole traders needing accounts to be drawn up and tax returns completed, through to large limited companies that require consultancy work.

XYZ clients include:

- Robert Fleece, a self-employed actor.
- Headly Style Ltd, a large fashion chain that manufactures its own garments in Asia and sells them in its network of stores in UK shopping malls.
- Hang Sen, a small takeaway food business.
- BigTown FC Ltd, a large, 'Premier league' football club.
- AxelAir Ltd, a small airline that charters its fleet of private jets to wealthy individuals.

You are Jasmine Miles, a student accountant that has recently joined XYZ. The position is your first job since leaving school.

Recently the following five matters have come to light.

BPP
LEARNING MEDIA

Matter 1

You have received the following email from Victoria Hills, the agent of Robert Fleece.

From: vhills@graceproductionsltd.co.uk
To: jasminemiles@xyz.co.uk
Subject: Robert Fleece Accounts and Tax Return

Hi Jasmine

Just to let you know that your uncle Robert's accounting records are on their way to you by courier. They consist of the following documents:

One folder containing his bank statements – Robert did his best to find them all but a large number are missing.

Expense receipts – there is a bag full of bus tickets, credit card receipts for meals and miscellaneous invoices for air fares and hotel accommodation for his holidays.

Job list – Robert has listed the work he has done this year and how much he was paid for each job.

Other information:

Robert is paid in cash for all his jobs and rarely pays the money into his bank account. Instead he uses the money to pay for his living expenses.

Robert asked me to remind you that due to financial difficulties he would really like to reduce his tax liability to below what he paid last year.

I know he is too polite to push you on this, but if you are unable to reduce his tax bill then I will report the matter to XYZ's senior partner who will take action against you.

I trust this is all the information that you need to draw up Robert's accounts and tax return for this year.

Regards

Victoria

[handwritten notes:]
- objective (uncle Rob) → familiarity
- integrity
- brief for behave
- intimidation (action)

Matter 2

You have been told that you will be on the team working on an assignment at Headly Style Ltd. In preparation for this, the senior partner has provided you with the following extracts from a recent newspaper article about the company.

Headly Style Ltd is a young company that has expanded rapidly over the last three years. Part of its success has been put down to the introduction of a code of conduct which is based on industry best practice and is aimed at preventing unethical and illegal behaviour by its employees.

However, the changes it has made have not been without issue. The business experienced a number of problems with its 'Movie Star' range of premium ladieswear when it emerged that materials used in the manufacturing process were of poor quality, resulting in many complaints from customers that the clothing tears easily and is not up to the standard they expect for the price they paid.

Perhaps more damaging was the scandal involving the company's 'Little Ripper' range of boyswear where an illegal dye was used in a batch of t-shirts resulting skin problems in a large number of children.

Adding to the company's woes, staff based in a number of the company's factories have taken to social networks, complaining about unethical behaviour by managers. Workplace bullying, compulsory overtime, poor working conditions and minimal breaks have all been mentioned, although the company insists the matter is greatly exaggerated.

Matter 3

The owner of the Hang Sen takeaway is wishing to retire and needs to dispose of her business. She has advertised the business for sale and wants XYZ to act for her to help achieve the best price possible.

Rather than pay for the work done on the usual rate-per-hour basis, she has asked whether she can arrange a fixed fee in advance, or whether the fee can be based on the sale price achieved by the practice. Due to uncertainties over the work, the practice cannot be sure how many hours the work will take, or the mix of junior and senior staff that will be required.

JP, an entrepreneur in the restaurant trade, has seen the Hang Sen takeaway advertised and has come to the practice for professional help in the buying process. He is particularly interested in obtaining the business for the lowest possible price.

Zac is another prospective buyer of the takeaway and has asked XYZ to become his accountant should he be successful in his bid to purchase the business. He is not currently a client of the practice.

Once the sale of the takeaway is complete, the current owner of the Hang Sen takeaway would no longer be a client of the firm.

Matter 4

You are involved in running the monthly payroll for BigTown FC. Last month was its year-end and you were asked to calculate the bonuses payable to the various departments.

Yesterday you received a call from a member of the club's marketing department. An excerpt of the conversation is as follows.

'..... thanks for all your hard work in calculating the annual bonuses, the marketing department is really happy with what they got and we would like to offer you and your father a day in our corporate hospitality box for the Cup Final....'

You are aware that your manager regularly socialises with players of BigTown FC and performs private taxation work for some of them. One afternoon the team's star player, Dwayne Looney, arrives at your office wanting to talk to your manager. He complains that the manager did not save him as much tax as one of the other players and tells him that he will take is business elsewhere unless he recalculates his tax to a lower amount.

Matter 5

The Chief Executive of AxelAir Ltd recently met with the senior partner of the practice. The Chief Exec is under pressure from the company's shareholders to improve the business's image concerning sustainability and has asked for assistance in forming a sustainability policy.

Task 5 (10 marks)

Refer to the Project Scenario and Matter 1.

(a) Explain which **THREE** fundamental principles are most threatened if you were to work on Robert Fleece's accounts and tax return.

(b) Explain **TWO** threats to fundamental principles that you face in this situation.

Task 6 (10 marks)

Refer to the Project Scenario and Matter 2.

(a) Explain what is meant by operational risk.

(b) Explain **TWO** examples of operational risk raised by the newspaper article.

(c) Explain the importance to Headly Style Ltd of its employees acting in accordance with its code of conduct rather than acting unethically or illegally.

Task 7 (10 marks)

Refer to the Project Scenario and Matter 3.

(a) Explain the fundamental ethical principle of objectivity.

(b) Explain whether or not charging the owner of the Hang Sen takeaway on a pre-arranged fee basis would be in breach of the fundamental ethical principles.

(c) Explain whether or not charging the owner of the Hang Sen takeaway on the basis of the value of the sale would be in breach of the fundamental ethical principles.

(d) Explain whether XYZ would be in breach of any fundamental principles by acting for JP in his prospective purchase of the takeaway.

(e) Explain whether XYZ would be in breach of any fundamental principles by taking on Zac as a client if he is successful in his prospective purchase.

Task 8 (10 marks)

Refer to the Project Scenario and Matter 4.

(a) **Explain whether you will breach any of your fundamental principles by accepting the hospitality.**

(b) **Whether or not there is a threat to your fundamental principles, explain what you should do in order to safeguard your position regarding the offer of hospitality.**

(c) **Explain TWO threats to the fundamental principles that your manager faces and what he should do to resolve each of them.**

••

Task 9 (10 marks)

Refer to the Project Scenario and Matter 5.

After the meeting with the Chief Exec of AxelAir Ltd, the senior partner has asked you to join the team working on the airline's sustainability policy. In particular, the senior partner has asked for your help on the following.

(a) **Explain what is meant by sustainability.**

(b) **Explain TWO sustainability policies relating to the airline and the environment.**

(c) **Explain TWO sustainability policies relating to the airline and society.**

••

BPP PRACTICE ASSESSMENT
PROFESSIONAL ETHICS

ANSWERS

PETH BPP practice assessment

Task 1

(a)   The correct answer is: The International Federation of Accountants (IFAC).

(b)   The correct answer is: The Serious Organisation Crime Agency (SOCA).

(c)   The correct answer is: Any two from breach of contract, professional negligence and breach of trust.

(d)   The correct answer is: Any two from, the Executive Committee, the Codes and Standards Committee and the Conduct Committee.

(e)   The correct answer is: Codes of conduct bring four main benefits to business organisations that introduce them.

   (1)   The standard of behaviour expected of employees is communicated to them effectively.

   (2)   The behaviour of employees becomes standardised or more consistent.

   (3)   The risk of unethical behaviour is reduced as employees who do not follow the code will 'stand out' and can be dealt with.

   (4)   Reputational risk for the organisation is reduced as behaviour becomes more ethical.

Task 2

(a)   The correct answer is: (1) Breach of contract, (2) Breach of trust, (3) Accusations of fraud and (4) Professional negligence.

(b)   The correct answer is: An accountant is expected to demonstrate the reasonable skill and care of a reasonable accountant. This level of skill might be increased if the accountant performs specialised work, or if they profess to have a higher level of skill than an average accountant.

(c)   The correct answer is: Compensation/damages.

(d)   The correct answer is: Professional competence and due care.

(e)   The correct answer is: Self-interest threat.

(f)   The correct answer is: Vanessa can add a disclaimer of liability to the reference.

(g)   The correct answer is, any two from the following: External audit, investment business and insolvency practice.

Task 3

(a) The correct answer is: The three safeguards are separation, use and accountability.

Separation – clients' monies should be held in accounts that are separate from each other and from those of the practice and the accountant.

Use – clients' monies should only be used for the purpose that they are intended.

Accountability – accountants should be ready at all times to account for their clients' monies, such as any income received from holding them and any payments made out of them.

(b) The correct answer is: Samantha should not agree to the client's request. An accountant should not hold funds if they suspect them to be criminal property. If the £10,000 is related to the client's potential fraud, it could be classified as criminal property and the practice should not hold it for the client.

Task 4

(a) The correct answer is: A professional accountant is permitted to disclose confidential information:

(1) Where they are properly authorised to do so and it is permitted by law;

(2) When they have a professional duty or right to do so, which is in the public interest and is not prohibited by law; and

(3) When they have a legal duty to do so.

(b) The correct answer is: Lana is in breach of the fundamental principle of confidentiality. The principle of confidentiality extends to staff under an accountant's authority.

Task 5

(a) Your fundamental principles that are most threatened are:

Integrity: The information being provided by Robert is clearly insufficient for you to produce accounts that accurately show his true financial position.

Objectivity: The threat to report you to the senior partner may be seen by others as an attempt by Victoria and Robert to influence your work.

Professional competence and due care: As a relatively new student accountant, you are not qualified to produce Robert's tax return.

(b) Two threats to your fundamental principles are:

Familiarity: Your close family relationship with Robert makes you potentially sympathetic to his interests.

Intimidation: You may be deterred from acting objectively due to the threat by Victoria to report you to the senior partner if Robert's tax liability is not reduced.

Task 6

(a) Operational risk is the risk of loss resulting from inadequate or failed internal processes, people and systems or from external events.

(b) Two examples of operational risk raised by the newspaper article:

Reputational risk – loss of reputation arising from the use of poor quality material in the expensive, 'premium' clothing range.

Litigation risk – legal action brought by the parents of the children affected by skin problems caused by the illegal dye.

(c) It is important that Headly Style Ltd's employees follow the code of conduct as it should reduce the operational risks it faces. It should also reduce the impact of the consequences of unethical and illegal behaviour that it may experience internally, such as reduced levels of employee performance and corporate productivity and increased employee turnover rates.

Task 7

(a) The fundamental principle of objectivity means that an accountant should do their work based on an independent and intellectually honest appraisal of information, their work should be free from prejudice and bias and free from all factors that might affect their impartiality.

(b) Charging the owner of the takeaway on a pre-arranged fee basis is likely to breach the fundamental ethical principles of professional competence and due care. This is because the practice cannot be certain how long the work will take, or what levels of staffing will be required. There is a risk of quoting a fixed price and then not being able to do the work with sufficient care and competence.

(c) A fee charged on a predetermined basis, relating to the outcome of a transaction is known as a contingent fee. They are permitted providing by doing so there is no threat to the fundamental ethical principles of professional competence and due care. In this instance there is no threat to the fundamental ethical principles because the practice can charge a fee based on the staff used and how long they work on the assignment.

(d) If XYZ were to act for JP then it would have a conflict of interest. This is because it would be trying to obtain the lowest possible sale price for JP and the highest possible sale price for the existing owner. If safeguards are not put in place, this would clearly be in breach of the fundamental principle of objectivity.

(e) Once the sale of the takeaway is complete and the current owner is no longer a client, there would be no reason why the firm could not take Zac on as a client. There would be no conflict of interest.

Task 8

(a) Accepting the hospitality would be in breach of the fundamental principle of objectivity as it could be seen as a reward from the marketing department for providing them with a good bonus.

(b) In order to protect your position you should notify your boss that the offer of hospitality has been offered to you.

(c) Your manager faces a familiarity threat caused by failing to maintain professional distance with the players of BigTown FC and an intimidation threat from Dwayne Looney in respect of the private taxation work.

The manager should cease socialising with the players and develop a professional distance from them. He should explain to Dwayne that taxation is dependent on personal circumstances and he cannot comment on the other player's tax matters due to client confidentiality. He should also say to Dwayne that if he is unhappy with his taxation work then he is free to look for another accountant.

•••

Task 9

(a) According to the UN's Brundtland Report, sustainability relates to the duty of businesses to protect society and future generations by considering them in the decisions taken today.

(b) Two sustainability policies relating to the airline and the environment.

The airline should invest in a modern fleet of aircraft that burn fuel efficiently and therefore lower the amount of pollution created.

Pilots should be encouraged to take the most fuel efficient routes and fly at the most economical speed to minimise the amount of fuel burned.

(c) Two sustainability policies relating to the airline and the society.

The airline should boost employment in the area in which it is based by hiring locally-based staff where possible.

The airline should consider the local community when deciding to fly at unsocial times of day (such as early in the morning or late at night) because the noise from aircraft might cause a disturbance.

•••

INDEX